Hathaway

THE GOOD FAIRY

THE GOOD FAIRY

A New Play

by

FERENC MOLNAR

Translated and Adapted by

JANE HINTON

Ray Long & Richard R. Smith, Inc.

New York · · · · 1932

PRINTED IN THE UNITED STATES OF AMERICA
BY J. J. LITTLE & IVES COMPANY, NEW YORK

As Presented at

HENRY MILLER'S THEATRE, New York

Beginning Monday Evening, November 30, 1931

GILBERT MILLER

Presents

HELEN HAYES

in

MOLNAR'S New Comedy

THE GOOD FAIRY

With

WALTER CONNOLLY

English Text by Jane Hinton, Settings by Joseph Urban.
Staged by Mr. Miller

CAST

(In the Order of Appearance)

THE HEAD WAITER	. . . .*Played by*	PAUL McGRATH
UNDERWAITER	"	" SALO DOUDAY
KONRAD	"	" EVELYN ROBERTS
LU	"	" HELEN HAYES
DR. METZ	"	" DOUGLAS WOOD
DR. SPORUM	"	" WALTER CONNOLLY
KAROLINE	"	" RUTH HAMMOND
LAW CLERK	"	" JACK LYNDS

ACT I. A private dining room in a hotel. Evening.

ACT II. Sporum's office. The next day.

ACT III. Sporum's office. The next afternoon.

EPILOGUE.

THE GOOD FAIRY

ACT I

CHARACTERS

Lu .... *25 years old*
Dr. Sporum .... *48 years old*
Konrad .... *45 years old*
Dr. Metz .... *48 years old*
Kellner .... *a head waiter, 32 years old*
Karoline .... *28 years old*
Manager

FIVE MUTE CHARACTERS

A Clerk
A Waiter
A Decorator
Two Workmen

THE GOOD FAIRY

ACT I

SCENE: *A private dining-room in a smart hotel.*
TIME: *Evening.*
AT RISE: *A table is set for three persons. There is champagne in an ice bucket. At rise of curtain the* HEAD WAITER *is bustling about in silence. Another* WAITER *enters with bottle of champagne in bucket. He uncorks champagne.* HEAD WAITER *at serving table. Suddenly* KONRAD *rushes into room. He gives coat to* WAITER. *He calls* HEAD WAITER *to him and proceeds to hurl orders at him wildly.*

KONRAD

[*To* WAITER.] Quick waiter—quick! Go to the side entrance immediately. There you will find a car with curtains drawn. In the car is a lady. Show her up here discreetly . . . without attracting any attention! Don't speak a word to her! Don't even say "good evening" and the moment she arrives—serve supper—at once.

[WAITER *takes his hat and exits.*]

[HEAD WAITER *listens attentively and then exits. There is a few moments' pause, during which* KONRAD *fusses about and picks up champagne bottle and looks at label, puts bottle on table.* LU *enters. She is in evening dress. She seems very*

[3]

excited. KONRAD *relieves her of her wrap. Both* LU *and* KONRAD *are obviously trying to put on the "grand manner."*]

LU

[*Smiles and presses hand to her heart.*] Oh, how my heart is beating!

KONRAD

But, Madame! What are you afraid of? Why this excessive caution? This game of hide and seek? This coming in separately instead of together?

LU

I must be so careful! . . . My husband! . . . Oh, my husband! If anyone sees me, I'm lost!

KONRAD

But I made the car stop in the side street. At the side entrance which leads directly to this room!

LU

You don't know my husband! He's terrifying! If I'm seen here alone, I can always say that I'm calling on a friend, who lives in this hotel. But, if I'm seen with a man . . . and just the two of us . . . then, Heaven protect me!

KONRAD

[*As the* WAITER *enters to serve hors d'oeuvres.*] Ah! Caviar à la Konrad. My own creation!
    [*The* WAITER *exits.*]

Lu

[*Goes to chair L. of table.*] Please—where is your friend? You said that your friend would be here, too! That was understood. It was absolutely understood that there would be three of us! You haven't lured me here under false pretenses have you?

Konrad

Oh, no. For Heaven's sake, calm yourself. You see there are three places. I was unable to reach the Minister in time. He had already arranged to attend a political dinner.

Lu

Oh.
[*With a start.*]

Konrad

But the dinner is being held in this hotel on the first floor. It's a banquet. And His Excellency has promised to divide his evening. He will join us later on. . . . This caution is fantastic. Are you afraid of me?

Lu

I . . . I . . . don't like to be alone . . . with a man . . . in a private room! I am not a tart!
[*Sits in chair L. of table*]

Konrad

[*Laughing.*] But all this excitement is nerve-wracking . . . every time we meet!
[*Sits in chair R. of table.*]

Lu

Now, now! "Every time?" This is only the third time we've met. The first time, at the dansant, where you and your friend, the Minister introduced yourselves . . . doesn't count! [*Coquettishly.*] Even then, you must have noticed, from the way I looked at you . . . that . . . although the Minister is a very fine looking man . . . I liked you best!

Konrad

[*Encouraged.*] Oh, sweet little Lu!
[Konrad *pours wine.*]

Lu

We have only met twice so far! Just count! This is the third time.

Konrad

And what fine times they were! The first, at three o'clock in the afternoon, in a crowded tea-room. The second also in the afternoon at a thé dansant! Always with a thousand people present!

Lu

You'll get used to it, my dear! What do you expect? You've hardly known me a week!

Konrad

Known you? That's an exaggeration. I only know that you are a lady, the wife of a lawyer, that much you have told me. Nothing else. You envelop yourself in mystery. I have told you everything about myself. You know that I was born here, and worked thirty years in South America. You haven't even told me your name.

LU

My name is Lu.

KONRAD

That's very little.

LU

Then—Luise.

KONRAD

That's a bit more, but still not enough.

LU

Isn't it more beautiful this way?

KONRAD

No.

LU

So romantic . . .

KONRAD

Why do you torture me with romance? Romance has been out of date for a long time. We live in a different age! Progress is the motto of our time. But . . . how shall I put it . . . there doesn't seem to be any noticeable progress between us!

Lu

Sir! This crude expression of impatience. . . .

Konrad

What do you intend to do with me? You can see that I love you, that I'm crazy about you! You're in my thoughts day and night. You interfere with my work —with my business—. Why are you here with me, if you don't love me?

Lu

Patience, patience!

Konrad

That's what you always say! How much longer . . .

Lu

I want to know you better. I'm not that kind of person. How often must I repeat that? I'm married. I have my scruples. For me, this is a most unusual experience! A . . . a tremendous experience! Not just a brief cynical adventure!

Konrad

Oh, charming, charming!
[*He makes a move towards her and sits in chair
back of table.*]

Lu

Now, now! Control yourself, President! Be a nice man and let's talk quietly. How much longer are you staying in Europe.

KONRAD

Oh, a long time. Perhaps a whole year. Until I have organized our branches all over Central Europe. That takes time.

LU

And then, you will return to . . . [*Sighs*] To your wife!

KONRAD

Yes. Why do you look at me so reproachfully? You have your husband. . . .

LU

Oh, my dear! Life is so horrible! Why does one always find the right man too late?

KONRAD

[*Rising and leaning over her.*] Lu! Lu! Lu! You drive me crazy when you talk like that!
[*He makes another move towards her.*]

LU

[*Pointing to chair R. of table.*] Please don't go crazy, President, it's so bad for you. . . .
[KONRAD *sits again R. of table.*]

KONRAD

Look here . . . I know that you can't fall in love with someone . . . on the spur of the moment. But I'm so nervous, because I feel that you are on the verge

[9]

of a decision. My happiness is a matter of days . . . or perhaps only hours.

Lu

Patience! We respectable women go at things more slowly. . . . You rich gentlemen are used to the tempo of fast women. You are spoiled, President!

Konrad

Oh, please don't say that! Especially, since you know that my love for you is based on respect. I love you because you are a lady, because this love is fraught with danger for both of us, because you are making a sacrifice!

Lu

Let's be frank! And because an open affair would damage your business reputation here and get you in trouble with your family.

Konrad

[*Laughing.*] Very clever! Very clever!

Lu

Oh yes! A society woman has her great advantages. We are discreet: we remain unseen, voila! [*Fan business.*] All that—is worth a little patience!

Konrad

[*Leaning back in chair.*] Yes, yes, of course. You talk so sensibly. It's a pleasure to listen to you. [*Leaning forward.*] Please forgive my . . . gross importunities. They are really due to the fact that I've been denied feminine society for a very long time. On the ship . . . not a single flirtation. And on my other journeys since then . . . not a single one! And now, I am suddenly thrown into your presence, for a whole week . . . your nearness, your perfume, your haunting voice . . . have all bewitched me, and yet . . .

Lu

You're too ardent, sir! Oh, much too ardent! Still, I like that! However, all you have said just now only concerns . . . shall I say . . . the physical?

Konrad

What worries me, too—you won't accept anything from me! I'd be so happy, if you would occasionally permit me to offer you a few trinkets. . . .

Lu

Sir!

Konrad

Yesterday, for instance, that beautiful ruby necklace in the shop window. . . .

Lu

President, these remarks are very distasteful!

Konrad

Well, it's something that you accept a few flowers!

Lu

Flowers, yes! But preferably only wild flowers!

Konrad

Oh!

Lu

There must not be the slightest relation between my eventual surrender [Konrad *starts*] and your financial status!

Konrad

What delicacy!

Lu

That's lucky, too, isn't it? Let's be frank about this, too! We are not expensive. That's another point in favor of us respectable women! [*Gesture from* Konrad.] Oh, I know, I know you're generous, sir! . . . Aren't you a lord?

Konrad

No. I am the President of a large corporation.

Lu

Oh, that's better than being a lord, isn't it?

Konrad

In our country . . .

Lu

And . . . in ours!

[12]

Konrad

I am a business man, Madame, and proud of it! I'm a business man.

Lu

I just dote on business men. I always bring them luck!

Konrad

That, too? Oh, you angel. [*Starts to take her hand, stops as* Kellner *enters with chicken and salad, crosses to serving table.*] Ah, here we are. Cold chicken and salad. And as far as luck is concerned, Madame, we'll soon see, for at this very moment, I'm waiting to hear the outcome of a very important business deal. I'm phoning later on to find out the result.

Lu

Really? Now, you've made me curious to see if I'll bring *you* luck!
  [Lu *exchanges glance with* Waiter.]

Konrad

[*To the* Waiter.] Bring me the telephone book.
  [Waiter *exits.*]

Lu

[*Looking over her shoulder at door. Frightened.*] Good Heavens!

Konrad

What is the matter?

Lu

That waiter knows me! . . . Oh, how awful! . . . It's just occurred to me! . . . I've dined here once or twice with my husband! . . . And now, that impudent waiter dares to smile at me! . . . Oh, I was a fool to come here! What *will* he think of me?

Konrad

Why should that matter to you?

Lu

I . . . I . . . don't like to be alone . . . with a man . . . in a private room! I'm not a tart! [*Nervously.*] What's happened to your friend? . . . And if I ever dine here again with my husband . . . that wretched waiter will be sure to grin at me!

Konrad

A waiter wouldn't do that!

Lu

Oh, I'm so nervous! . . . Oh, how nervous I am! [*Nervously.*] Please, give me a cigarette.

Konrad

With pleasure. [*Takes out cigarette case and leaves it on the table.*] Extra special! [*He lights her cigarette.*] Made especially for me in Egypt!

Lu

Especially for you?

KONRAD

Especially for me.

LU

What an extravagance! [*Puffing cigarette.*] Your friend, the Minister, is a fine looking man. And he seems to be a gentleman, too.

KONRAD

He is a perfect gentleman, Madame.

LU

He inspires confidence. His appearance is very distinguished. His manners are charming. But I can't wait for him very much longer. I lied to my husband. I told him I was going to the theatre with a girl friend—— [KONRAD *starts.*] Oh my friend can be trusted. She goes to the theatre alone and then afterwards, over the telephone, she tells me about the play, so that I can talk to my husband about it . . . oh, yes. A single woman doesn't need to complicate her life with lies. . . . But we married women are slaves to them. [*Nervously.*] My position here is intolerable. . . . Oh that waiter. . . . Go and fetch the Minister. [*Irritably.*] At once.

> [WAITER *enters with telephone directory.* KONRAD *rises and takes it.* WAITER *crosses above table to* KONRAD, *is about to exit, when* KONRAD *calls him.*]

KONRAD

Wait a minute, please. [*Takes the directory.*] You must get me the number.

Lu

[*Nervously.*] Please, don't bother about business now! My honor is at stake! Go and fetch him here!
  [*Takes the directory away from him and crosses towards sofa.*]

Konrad

[*Laughing.*] Well done, little tyrant! Dictator, Dictatress, Mussolina!

Lu

I hope you don't mind, President! Au revoir!

Konrad

[*In the doorway.*] Madame, I highly appreciate the psychological import of your remark and I am happy to conform thereto!
  [Konrad *exits. Brief pause.* Lu *sits. The* Waiter *walks to* Lu's *table, fills a glass with champagne, sits on table and drinks it calmly. He and* Lu *then begin a hurried, whispered duologue.*]

Waiter

Why all the elegant talk?

Lu

I'm not talking. I'm making conversation. Please, don't give me away! I told him I was a lady . . . a society lady!

Waiter

And why are you so cautious? Why are you playing hide and seek?

Lu

That's why! So that he'll believe I'm a lady! I told him I was the wife of a lawyer!

WAITER

Why did you say that?

Lu

So that he'll respect me! . . . Say! What does "psychological import" mean?

WAITER

The way you think about something.

Lu

And what does "conform" mean?

WAITER

To do as you're told!

Lu

Thanks.

WAITER

The dress?

Lu

Borrowed.
  [*Weeps.*]

WAITER

Why are you crying?

Lu

Please, don't give me away!

Waiter

Oh! What do you think I am? [*Pause.*] I haven't seen you for a long time.

Lu

I don't come here for tea any more. Do I owe you much?

Waiter

That's unimportant.

Lu

You are a gentleman.

Waiter

[*Finishing his champagne.*] Always.

Lu

You'll get your money . . . [*Pause.*] Do you still love me?

Waiter

[*Crossing to serving table.*] *Still.* How long have you known him?

Lu

A week.

Waiter

Do you love him?

Lu

No. I don't love him, but he . . . shall we say . . . he pleases me. Or shall we say . . . he doesn't please me.

Waiter

Well then——

Lu

Only he's too important. . . . Rich and in love. But there's been nothing between us, so far. . . . We have only danced . . .

Waiter

The tango?

Lu

Yes.

Waiter

Well, that's a beginning. . . .

Lu

Don't make fun of me. I don't love him. But he loves and respects me . . . like a married lady! That's what his love is based on! Respect. That's why he treats me so nicely! You see, again tonight, he has brought me to a fashionable place! If he knew that I'm only a movie usherette. . . . A sort of glow worm . . . with my flashlight blinking in the dark . . . all dressed in lemon yellow coat and glaring red skirt. . . . What did you just tell me? What does "psychological import" mean?

WAITER

The way you think about something.

LU

And what was that other one? . . . Oh, yes . . . "conform!"

WAITER

To do as you're told.

LU

Thanks.

WAITER

Why do you ask?

LU

I like to learn.

WAITER

[*Crossing to centre table.*] You watch out that some day he doesn't wander into the movie theater.

LU

Oh, I left the movie theater a week ago. For his sake. He respects me so!

WAITER

How do you know that he respects you?

LU

He doesn't give me money! But don't worry . . . I wouldn't take it anyway . . . I won't sell my-self.

WAITER

Then—what do you live on?

LU

Oh, I eat a lot of cakes at the dansants! And then, I've saved a little . . . enough for two weeks. . . . And I have debts, too! . . . Nice, big ones!

WAITER

Debts! Who would give you credit?
[*Sits at table.*]

LU

Everybody! Everybody likes me! [*Sadly.*] That's why I have so many debts! [*She drinks.*] Board bills, dressmakers, shoemakers, hairdressers, manicures, sleeping-powders, permanent waves, reducing tablets, dentists, cigarettes, Eau de Cologne, powder, rouge, magazines, dog license . . . all on credit! There's only one person to whom I pay cash . . .

WAITER

Who?

LU

The beggar. [*Drinks.*] That's because I expect that some day he'll have to support me. So far, I've never been able to sell myself. [*With great determination.*] But now . . . I'm going to gather all my strength and try it. I'm so unhappy.

WAITER

You're tight.

Lu

Yes, a teeny-weeny bit. Why do you look at me like that?

Waiter

I'm not looking at you *like that*.

Lu

I really am to be pitied, am I not?

Waiter

You are.

Lu

I'm not in the story.

Waiter

What story?

Lu

Life! I'm always the next installment.

Waiter

You're what?

Lu

The next installment. And when the next installment arrives . . . I'm the one after that! I'm a peninsula.

Waiter

A peninsula?

Lu

Yes! Like a peninsula, I reach out from the old life into the new . . . but never succeed in breaking away.

WAITER

That's clever.

LU

I don't know what I am. What do you think? Am I a tart?

WAITER

No.

LU

I don't think so, either. Am I a working girl? [WAITER *tries to speak*.] No . . . and yet, that would be my ideal! But, I can't work.

WAITER

Too bad.

LU

I can't work. Maybe I am a tart, after all?

WAITER

I've already told you—No!

LU

I'm unable to sell myself for money. And yet, that would be my ideal! But I just can't!

WAITER

Well then, what are you doing here with this . . .

LU

I've already told you. I want to have one last try. He's very rich. And I can't go on like this any longer.

[23]

But it's so hard. I keep putting it off like a visit to the dentist's. It's dreadful! . . . I'd rather starve than have anything to do with a man I don't love . . . I don't matter that much. . . . On the other hand, you know . . . for the sake of my poor, sick, little mother . . . I could even walk the streets! But I haven't got one! . . . Or, if I had a child. . . . Then I could rip the heart out of a rich man's body! But, I have no one! [*Drying her tears.*] What's the use of talking? I can't . . . for money! [*Weeping.*] I can't . . . with a man I don't love!

WAITER

What are you crying about? That's a very beautiful sentiment.

LU

Nowadays? . . . It's a disease!

WAITER

What?

LU

I've already seen a doctor about it!

WAITER

And what did he say?

LU

A change of air . . . and lots of vitamins! [*Weeps bitterly.*]

WAITER

Don't cry.

LU

[*Pause.*] Do you know what I'd like to be?

WAITER

What?

LU

An idiot. They say idiots are happy.

WAITER

Do you think you're so wise?

LU

No. But I'm not an idiot, either! Fifty-fifty. And that's the worst of all! But—God loves me. . . .

WAITER

That's a lot!

LU

Because I'm good. Am I not?

WAITER

Oh, yes.

LU

I do good whenever I can. Do you know what I am?

WAITER

What?

LU

A fairy!
  [*She drinks.*]

[25]

WAITER

Don't drink so much. It makes you conceited.

LU

Don't say that. If I hadn't that illusion . . . I'd have eaten a pound of Aspirin long ago! Besides I've brought you luck, too!

[*Rising and crossing to sofa.*]

WAITER

When?

LU

Tonight. There's going to be a huge bill tonight. That's lucky for you, isn't it?

[*Getting handbag and starting to repair make-up.*]

WAITER

[*Rising.*] Yes. That's lucky for me.

LU

So, I'm a useful member of society after all! Am I not?

WAITER

Oh, you are!

LU

Only . . . I'm a "member-in-bad-standing," I suppose you'd say?

WAITER

I'm afraid so.

Lu

I have no one. Have I?

Waiter

If you say so. And if you don't count me.
[Lu *pulls something out of the corner of her chair.
She shows it to* Waiter.]

Lu

What is this?

Waiter

Good Lord! Baron Hell's gold cigarette case! We've
been hunting for it all week. I've even been to the po-
lice about it! Where was it?

Lu

Right here. It had slipped down in the corner.

Waiter

You darling! You can't imagine how happy you've
made me! They even suspected me!

Lu

[*Looks at* Waiter *and goes to table*.] Now, you see?
I found it without even looking for it!

Waiter

You really *are* a fairy!

Lu

Oh, I am!
> [*Serious.*]
> [*Puts some of* KONRAD'S *cigarettes into the Baron's case.*]

WAITER

What are you doing?

Lu

Performing a little miracle. What is the name of the baron who lost this?

WAITER

Baron Hell.

Lu

Well, let Baron Hell have a little extra special happiness. A few extra special cigarettes. A little present from the fairy.

WAITER

A present? But, you're stealing them, my dear child! You're stealing them from someone else!

Lu

When one can do good, one shouldn't hesitate at a little sin!
> [*Gives him the case. They laugh.* WAITER *kisses her hair.* KONRAD *enters. He doesn't see the kiss, but notices that they are smiling.*]

WAITER

[*Going to serving table.*] Would Madame care for some mineral water?

Lu

[*Very aristocratic.*] Thank you, waiter,—no!
[*Picking up fan.*]

Waiter

[*Puts the bottle away.*] Very well, Madame.

Konrad

The Minister will be here shortly. Your command has
been duly executed, Madame!

Lu

[*With exaggerated refinement.*] I'm very grateful,
President. Pray forgive me, for having troubled you.
You see, these fears and precautions are the disadvan-
tages of us society women. But what can we do? We
must . . . conform . . . to the psychological imports
. . . of our husband's wishes. Ahh!
[*She sighs triumphantly at her elegant speech.*
Waiter *smiles.*]

Konrad

Will you permit me to make my telephone call now?
[*He goes to sofa and picks up phone directory.*]

Lu

I was just going to ask you to . . .

KONRAD

[*Looks for the number in telephone directory. Speaks to* WAITER.] Will you get me 181-92. And if no one answers there, try 949-49.

[WAITER *writes down the numbers and exits.*]

KONRAD

That waiter really did smile at you . . . rather meaningly. And . . . as a matter of fact . . . you didn't look at him any too severely. [*Moving to her.*] Quite good-looking . . . for a waiter!

LU

What does this mean, President? Are you jealous of a waiter?

KONRAD

Of every man, Madame! And particularly of this one! I don't know why . . . but I'm particularly jealous of this one!

LU

[*Holding fan at side.*] But, sir! He belongs to a totally different social class!

KONRAD

Never mind. Anything can happen in this world!

LU

How ardent you are! . . . And what wild imagination! But how interesting!

KONRAD

[*A step to her.*] Oh Lu . . . Lu . . . Lu . . . I'm going crazy. You're so divine!
[*He tries to embrace her.*]

LU

No—No! [*Pushes him into chair. Moves away from him.*] Sit down like a nice man, and have something to eat. You've hardly eaten anything.

KONRAD

That's what love does to me.
[Lu *serves from serving table; then sits back of table.*]

LU

A little cold chicken. This cold supper is very wholesome, my dear President. It contains heaps of calories and vitamins, but still it isn't fattening. Do you like vitamins?

KONRAD

I adore them!

LU

So do I. Have you ever seen a vitamin?

KONRAD

No.

LU

Neither have I.
[*They eat.*]

[31]

KONRAD

I'm happy the supper pleases you!
[*Pours champagne.*]

LU

Pleases me! . . . That's putting it mildly! You know how to appreciate the good things of life! My dear President. You're an epi-epi-cur-ist!

KONRAD

Oh Lu! . . . what thrilling words!
[*He moves his chair nearer and tries to embrace her.*]

LU

[*She reaches out and pushes him slowly.*] No—no! Be quiet, sir! Let's eat!
[*She eats.*]

KONRAD

Didn't you tell me that you were on a reducing diet?

LU

Yes. But there is one rule for every reducing diet.

KONRAD

What is it?

LU

It starts tomorrow!
[*She eats.*]

[32]

KONRAD

Oh, Lu. . . .
　[*Moves his chair; tries to embrace her again.*]

LU

Now stop that, please! Don't be so grabby. [*Points to chair R. of table.*] It's high time His Excellency arrived.

KONRAD

[*Sits R. of table.*] I warn you—His Excellency is a little er—drunk.

LU

Oh that's all right! I like them like that!

KONRAD

Let us drink too.

LU

With pleasure, President.
　[*They drink.*]

KONRAD

[*Moving his chair nearer the table.*] And now, darling, tell me about yourself. What is your name? Where do you live? How do you live? You are so shy! . . . so mysterious! Where do you spend your evenings? Do you go to the movies often?

LU

There was a time when I went every night. But not now.

KONRAD

I hope you don't mind my asking you these questions. But you are not just a fleeting adventure to me, you know.

LU

What do you love about me?

KONRAD

Everything—your charm—your enchantingly aristocratic manner which, if I may say so, is in such striking contrast to your—your bubbling personality.

LU

Does my personality really bubble?

KONRAD

Like champagne, dear lady! It intoxicates me. . . . I must know who you are . . . and I should also like to ask you most respectfully about your financial status.

LU

Fair.

KONRAD

Have you a car?

LU

No.

KONRAD

Furs——

LU

No.

KONRAD

Jewels?

LU

No! . . . These questions are very distasteful. One can easily see you're not a lord. I'm not a tart. What would my husband say if he saw me wearing costly presents?

KONRAD

Your husband's a lawyer?

LU

Oh . . . yes!

KONRAD

As I've already told you, I am now engaged in organizing the Central European branches of my firm. I am greatly in need of a good lawyer, so that if . . .

LU

President, that's a plain financial proposition!

KONRAD

[*In a business-like manner.*] But look here—forgive my saying this, but I hate successful lawyers. Once they are rich and famous they don't care a hang for anything! What we want is a good, hard-working lawyer! Really, you'd be doing me a favor if you'd help me find one.

Lu

Do you mean it?

Konrad

I'd be very grateful to you . . . oh, they're only *small* cases but quite a lot of them. . . . I won't go into details; it would only bore you. . . . It is sufficient to say that it means a very large but assured income.

Lu

And it all depends on you?

Konrad

Entirely! I can make someone rich with the stroke of my pen!

Lu

It sounds like a fairy tale!

Konrad

It's real, nevertheless. And it wouldn't be a present either . . . he'd have to work for it!

Lu

And it wouldn't be your money.

Konrad

You are right! It would be the firm's money. [*Coaxingly.*] Why should I let it go to others . . . strangers? . . . Wouldn't that mean everything for you: a car, jewels, furs?

Lu

Oh, my husband would shower me with presents. He's so generous!

Konrad

But won't you tell me now, who is your husband?

Lu

When you have earned my confidence I will tell you everything.

[*The* Waiter *enters and crosses above table to R. of* Konrad.]

Waiter

I've got your number at last, sir. The first number didn't answer, but 949-49 is now on the wire.

[*Goes to fetch the grapes on the little table and offers them to* Lu.]

Konrad

[*Rises, crosses to door.*] You'll excuse me, Madame, won't you?

Lu

Certainly! I'm dying to hear if I brought you luck or not! . . . What's this? Oh, grapes! And so out of season too! You will spoil me, President.

[Waiter *to below R. of chair R.*]

Konrad

That's my one ambition!
[*Exits.*]

[37]

Lu

[*Rises. Looks after him and crosses excitedly to door, then back to* WAITER.] A name, a name of a lawyer, quickly.

WAITER

What for?

Lu

He wants to know my husband's name! Give me a name!

WAITER

Invent one.

Lu

Oh no! I must have a real one! We've got a chance to make someone happy!

WAITER

How's that?

Lu

He wants to make my husband rich!

WAITER

But you haven't got a husband, have you?

Lu

That's why I'm asking you for a name, idiot! Quickly! He's just crazy to make my husband rich! Quickly! Name me a lawyer! I tell you we've got a chance to make someone very happy!

[38]

WAITER

What a crazy idea! Anybody could see that you've been drinking.

LU

[*Walking L. and back.*] Well, it's a good thing I have been drinking. Now that I've decided to surrender at least someone is going to profit by it. Sweetheart, who's *your* lawyer?

WAITER

He doesn't deserve it!

LU

I don't know any lawyers at all, thank goodness! But quickly!—Let's take one from the telephone book! [*She crosses to sofa, he follows her; she grabs the book from sofa.*] We will open it anywhere and the first lawyer on the page will be the lucky one! [*Opens the book. They bend over it, searching and whispering "s-s-s."*] I've got him! Here he is! Sporum, Max, 104 Weisenburgerstrasse, Telephone 911-19.

WAITER

Don't know him.

LU

Neither do I! [WAITER *jots down the name and number.*] But I'll make him rich—I will.

WAITER

What if he is rich already?

Lu

Then he won't get anything. But I'm sure he's poor. Don't worry—I only make mistakes when I think. When I do something blindly I always hit the mark! I bet that he's the poorest lawyer in the whole city! I'm either a good fairy or I'm not.

Waiter

What if he's married?

Lu

Then he'll never know how it all happened. His good fortune will have just dropped from heaven!

Waiter

And if——

Lu

Don't ask so many questions. I haven't any use for logic. [*Crosses to R. and hides note in dress.*] There we are: I'm so excited, I'm so happy! [*Chimes ring out. She goes to window.*] Oh! Isn't it lovely! It's midnight now and somewhere a poor man lies asleep in his bed and doesn't even dream that at this very moment he is rich. Don't you see? That's how a good fairy works!

Waiter

You ought to get a commission.

Lu

Oh! A good fairy and a commission!

WAITER

That happens very often.

LU

No! I'm performing miracles, not taking profits!

WAITER

Well, I hope it turns out all right. [*Then as* KONRAD *enters radiantly, the* WAITER *goes to serving table.*] Mineral water, Madame?

LU

Thank you, Waiter, no!
[WAITER *replaces bottle.*]

WAITER

Very well, Madame.

LU

[*To* KONRAD, *giving him her hands.*] Well, I can see by your face . . . It was good news!

KONRAD

[*Crossing below table to chair R. of table. Happily.*] Oh, and what good news, dear lady! My men have won all along the line! Or to put it more plainly, we had hoped to conclude a deal involving a million and it has turned out to be a million and a half!
[*Sits R. of table.*]

LU

Oh, President, I'm so glad!

KONRAD

You're a mascot, Lu! Let's drink to it. [WAITER *starts to pour the wine from front of table*.] Never mind, my friend, you may go. I'll attend to that! [*Exit* WAITER *looking back at* LU.] Remarkable, the way that waiter always manages to be *in* when I'm *out!*

LU

Sir?

KONRAD

I hate that waiter! But don't let's bother about him now. [*They both drink*.] Where were we? Oh yes! You were at last going to tell me who is your husband? What is his name?

LU

You will make him rich?

KONRAD

I will . . . at once!

LU

Promise?

KONRAD

I promise!

LU

Oh, the great moment has come! Shall I or shall I not?

KONRAD

Please, I beg you to!

LU

Dr. Max Sporum.

KONRAD

At last! [LU *sits R. of table. He jots down the name.*] His address? He's in the phone book, isn't he?

LU

He most certainly *is!*

KONRAD

[*Going to back of her chair.*] Well, you will have no reason to complain of me, little girl . . . tomorrow you will hear from me . . . I'm a man of my word . . . and by this time tomorrow the contract will have been signed!

LU

Only, for heaven's sake, go about it cleverly! You mustn't say you know me!

KONRAD

That goes without saying, my dear. I'm a gentleman.

LU

You say that a little too often, President! But no matter . . . oh dear, if only Max doesn't suspect . . . I'm sure he'd strangle me!

KONRAD

Nonsense, Madame! Nonsense! I'll say he was recommended to me by the Embassy!

[43]

Lu

And not a word about knowing me!

Konrad

But my dear lady, I'm a gentleman . . . I mean to say, I give you my word of honor! Won't that suffice?

Lu

Oh, yes! That'll suffice. Thank you, President, I'm so happy that I can make Max happy!

Konrad

[*Taking her hand.*] And I am so happy that I can make *you* happy!

[*Kisses her hand.*]

Lu

[*Delighted.*] Oh, aren't we having a lovely chat?

Konrad

[*Overjoyed, puts his arm around her, goes down on one knee.*] At last you are beginning to enjoy yourself! Now, the Minister need not come at all, eh?

Lu

[*Coquettishly.*] You're right. Now that I have had a little to drink, I have more courage! You are so good to me, you dear man!

[*They move towards each other. The* Waiter *enters, stands R. of door.*]

[44]

WAITER

[*Announces.*] His Excellency, Dr. Metz!
  [KONRAD *and* LU *rise.*]
  [*The* MINISTER *reels in drunkenly, in evening dress. He bows deeply.* WAITER *exits.*]

LU

[*Crossing to* METZ.] Sir, you have kept a lady waiting!

METZ

A thousand pardons, Madame.
  [*Kisses her hand.*]

LU

[*Sitting back of table.*] Sit down, and eat and drink and make conversation.

METZ

[*Sways, as he sits down chair L. of table.*] Thank you!
  [KONRAD *sits R. of table.*]

LU

On the chair, Your Excellency—not next to it!

METZ

Thanks for that most practical bit of advice.

LU

I understand that you are drunk, Dr. Metz?

[45]

Metz

That is a fact, Madame.

Lu

Well, I'm surprised at you . . . a Minister. . . .

Metz

We are only human.

Lu

Oh, absolutely! Do you mind telling me where you minister?

Metz

At the Ministry, of course!

Lu

You don't say! And what do you do there?

Metz

I am the Minister of *Futilities*. [*Laughs.*] I'm the man who decides who is to have a title and who is not. *Old titles which must be handed down carefully, and new ones which can be bought!*

Lu

And all that depends on you?

[46]

Metz

It does. And what's more, it's very delicate work. I am said to be the most tactful cabinet minister in existence!

Lu

You must be a very powerful man. But I'll bet that you're a severe one, too.

Metz

I should say I am! But those who are nice to me—you charming lady—those who are nice to me can have anything that they want.

[*He tries to embrace her.*]

Lu

Sir! This is indeed a painful surprise! Are you trying to paw me?

Metz

That *has* been done!

Konrad

Steady, Metz, steady!

Metz

What? You're not jealous, Konrad, are you?

Lu

Of course he is! He's terribly jealous! And you mustn't forget that you are a very handsome man.

[47]

KONRAD

But Madame . . .

METZ

Am I intruding?

LU

No, no! We were just having a chat.

METZ

What about, may I ask?

LU

We were talking about my husband.

METZ

Oh, that interests me too. Who wouldn't be interested in the lucky man who owned such a jewel? Ah, what eyes, what hands, what legs, what breasts. . . .

LU

[*Interrupting.*] Your Excellency! What lewd language!

KONRAD

[*To* METZ.] My dear friend, I must really ask you to adopt another tone in speaking to this lady. It happens that she *is* a lady. She is the wife of a distinguished lawyer!

METZ

Oh!

Lu

Of course I am! What did you think I was?

Metz

[*Laughing loudly.*] Shan't tell you!

Lu

Well, if you are the most tactful of ministers, I can just imagine what the others are like!

Metz

And what sort of man is your most fortunate husband? What does he look like?

Lu

[*Crisply.*] Handsome——

Metz

Young or old?

Lu

Older than I and younger than you.

Metz

Tall or short?

Lu

Taller than a thimble and shorter than a skyscraper.
[*Laughing.*]

Metz

What's the color of his hair? Dark or fair?

Lu

Well, let's see. How can I describe it. Well, it's attractive——

Metz

[*With a drunken laugh.*] That's a new color . . . attractive—ha, ha. And tell me, does Mr. Attractive know Mr. Konrad as yet?

Lu

No.

Metz

But he is a very good person for a lawyer to know! Can Mr. Attractive boast of many acquaintances as worthwhile as Mr. Konrad?

[Metz *laughs.*]

Lu

Please, Mr. President, protect me! The Minister of Futilities is being tactless!

Konrad

[*His arm around her.*] Excellency, I humbly beg your pardon. Madame is so sensitive, you must be careful how you speak to her, or she will wilt like a flower.

Lu

He is rude enough to wilt an oak.

Konrad

Really, Madame, this is very painful to me! I am very sorry, very sorry.

METZ

Tell me, is this the way Mr. Attractive makes all his worthwhile acquaintances?

LU

This is outrageous! Stop it, please! President, protect me!

KONRAD

Your Excellency!

METZ

[*Stammering.*] Mr. Attractive—Mr. Thimble—Mr. Skyscraper——

LU

[*Very angry, a little drunk.*] I won't have you make fun of my husband! It's insulting! You ought to be ashamed of yourself!

KONRAD

[*Hopping to and fro in consternation.*] Please, Madame! Excellency . . . Madame . . . Excellency. . . .
   [WAITER *enters and whispers to* LU.]

WAITER

Don't get excited, Lu.

LU

[*Rising; screaming.*] I demand that my husband be respected! I demand it!

[51]

KONRAD

[*Rises.*] But Madame—before the waiter. . . .

LU

Before the waiter or behind the waiter, it's all the same to me! I go crazy when anyone insults my husband!

METZ

But Madame. I . . . I . . . I . . .
[*Rising to bow, but falls back in chair. He is unable to continue for laughing.*]

LU

[*Angrily. Going to sofa and getting her things.*] Go home and sleep it off! [*To the* WAITER.] Waiter, get me a taxi! [*To* KONRAD.] President, get your bill! I am not going to stay here and listen to my husband being slandered!

METZ

But my dear Madame, I am really sorry. I regret extremely . . .

LU

[*Turns to* METZ.] Oh, go to the devil!

KONRAD

[*To the* WAITER.] Let me have my bill, please.

LU

[*Calls after the* WAITER.] And a taxi! [WAITER exits. LU goes D. R. LU flares up again.] I am not going to have my husband slandered! [*Thumping her fist on the table.*] I am not going to have it! [*Hurls a glass against the door.*] I am not going to . . .

KONRAD

But dear lady, there will be a scandal!

LU

I don't care! I won't have my poor dear husband treated like that! At this very moment he is sitting at home . . . at his desk . . . working his fingers to the bone for me, and you . . . here . . . [*Sobs wildly.*] . . . dare to insult him . . . and make fun of him. . . .

METZ

[*Rises.*] Well, there's nothing for me to do but leave! That *may* clear the air. [*Walks to the door.*] I bid you good night. And please don't forget to invite me to your next jolly little party!
[*Leaves offended.*]

LU

[*As* METZ *exits.*] Can you imagine that? Now *he's* been insulted!

KONRAD

And my title is off for at least another year!

LU

I could have boxed his ears for him!

KONRAD

Coming from you even that must be sweet.

LU

I'd advise you not to try it, President!
[LU *rises*.]

WAITER

[*Enters. To table*.] Your bill, sir. [*To* LU.] The taxi will be here in a moment, Madame.

KONRAD

[*R. of* WAITER. *Looking at the bill*.] Waiter, this bill is outrageous!

WAITER

Outrageous? What do you mean, sir?

KONRAD

I don't usually say anything, but this is much too much. 120 marks for caviar!

LU

Mr. President, that isn't done.

KONRAD

Oh, I beg your pardon!
[*He pays angrily with two notes. The* WAITER *exits with the money*.]

Lu

[*Nervously.*] And now you must go first. . . . We must leave as we came.

Konrad

[*Goes down to her.*] But what's the use of all this . . . this . . .

Lu

Please don't make me nervous. Do as I tell you! I must be so careful! Can't you ever understand that? Poor Maxie is so jealous!
[*At the mention of the name of "Max" she again breaks out in tears.*]

Konrad

And when will I see you again, darling?

Lu

Tomorrow.

Konrad

At what time?

Lu

At ten o'clock . . . like tonight. . . . Call for me at the tea room, but don't come in. Send your chauffeur.

Konrad

Thank you . . . thank you. And then may I hope that tomorrow—please, answer me!

[55]

Lu

Oh, darling!
[*She falls into his arms. There is a long passionate kiss.*]

Konrad

The first kiss! Oh, Lu . . . Lu . . . I'm going mad! I'm going mad!

Lu

[*Pushing him away.*] No, don't go mad. . . . Just go! . . . Go quickly! . . . that's best.
[*Waiter enters, crossing below table to L. of Konrad.*]

Waiter

The taxi is here, Madame. [*Offers Konrad his change on the tray.*] Your change, sir.

Konrad

So! I get something back after all, eh? I'm surprised!

Lu

[*To Konrad, as he reaches for it.*] Leave it, President. [*To the Waiter, very grandly.*] That's for you, Waiter.

Waiter

Thank you, Madame.
[*Goes to table and busies himself.*]

Lu

And now . . . once again, President. Adieu!

[56]

KONRAD

[*Kisses her hand.*] Permit me to apologize for the Minister's behavior.

[KONRAD *exits, kissing hand to* LU.]

WAITER

The Minister is rather common.

LU

Very common! [*Smiles.*] But he has made me happy!

WAITER

But you were crying!

LU

With happiness! It was so good to defend someone, to belong to someone . . . I cried so beautifully . . . I'm so grateful to the Minister for having insulted poor Max.

WAITER

[*Coming down.*] If Max knew about this he would probably give you a good beating.

LU

I don't care! I need Max . . . Oh, I've got such a big heart and no one to put in it! [*Moving to him.*] I'm so lonely . . . so lonely . . .

[57]

WAITER

You can have me, Lu.
[*A step nearer to her.*]

LU

What, again! Don't be silly! I can't . . . now!

WAITER

Have you arranged to meet him tomorrow?

LU

Yes.

WAITER

Then you finally decided . . .

LU

Well . . . half and half . . . you never can tell . . .
though I do think I'll succeed this time . . . for now
I'll be helping my little Maxie. Why do you look at me
like that?

WAITER

I am *not* looking at you *like that*.

LU

Does it hurt you to think about it?

WAITER

Can't deny it.

LU

[*Nearer to him.*] Oh dear, you are a good friend.

[58]

WAITER

[*By chair L. of table. Back to audience.*] A better friend than you think.

LU

The very best!

WAITER

I'd like to marry you, Lu.

LU

But not *now*, you foolish boy, not now!

WAITER

[*Arm around Lu's shoulder.*] I've been offered a nice little place in the suburbs . . . One could almost call it a first-class restaurant . . . there you could have a clean, respectable, quiet life . . . a little house . . . a bit of a garden . . . and babies . . .

LU

[*Looking up at him.*] How many babies?

WAITER

One every year.

LU

Oh, that's always been my ideal! But unfortunately this isn't the time for it. Please, please, don't try to ruin my career! [THE WAITER *kisses her hand and laughs softly.*] Why do you kiss my hand?

WAITER

Because I'm grateful to you for having made me rich.
[*Shows her the bill.*] And because you found the gold
cigarette case.

LU

I'm so glad I did!

WAITER

[*Whispers.*] May I take you home?

LU

No. . . . What are you thinking of?
[WAITER *hangs his head.*]

LU

Don't despair . . . Wait and have patience . . .
Your time will come . . . Don't worry . . . I shan't
let you suffer . . . I shan't let anybody suffer . . .
Give me my wrap. [*The* WAITER *goes to sofa, takes
the wrap and comes to her.*] The Minister will make
Max a Judge. I'll speak to him about it. [WAITER
helps her into her wrap.] Oh, Maxie is gently sleeping
somewhere in the distance. Somewhere in this big
city . . . in the night . . . and doesn't know that tomorrow he'll be rich . . . rich and envied . . . Oh
. . . I'm too happy for words. I shan't be able to sleep
all night. Kiss my hand again.

[*She holds out her hand.*]

WAITER

Again?

LU

Yes! I don't know why . . . I feel like it tonight. . . . That's right. [*She walks to the door smiling.*] And now . . . [*The door opens slowly.*] Adieu!
[*She slips through the door. The door closes.*]

CURTAIN

THE GOOD FAIRY

ACT II

ACT II

SCENE: MAX SPORUM'S *office. It is a simple, shabby office. On the left two doors leading to his living quarters. At the right main entrance.*

TIME: *The next day.*

AT RISE: *At rise of curtain* SPORUM *is seated at a small table, with his back toward the audience. He is finishing his mid-day meal, eating pickled pork, and drinking beer.* MISS KAROLINE *serves him and stands beside him while he eats.*

SPORUM *is forty-eight years old, very neat and pompous, with a Van Dyke beard.* KAROLINE *is his secretary and chief-clerk in one. She is a pretty, energetic person, deeply attached to* SPORUM.

SPORUM

[R. C. *back to audience.*] I'm not even looking at you, Miss Karoline, and yet I know what you're thinking.

KAROLINE

[*Above table R. C.*] Well, what am I thinking, Mr. Sporum?

SPORUM

You're thinking what you always think at lunchtime, that a lawyer ought to be ashamed of himself if

[65]

at the age of forty-eight he can't afford anything better than beer and pickled pork.

KAROLINE

Money doesn't bring happiness, Mr. Sporum.

SPORUM

That's true enough. Money never brought me happiness. But then, it never tried to. Still, I believe it could, if it ever tried. [*Stands up and walks to desk which faces the audience. Lights a cigar.*] May I have a cup of coffee, Miss Karoline?

KAROLINE

We haven't any coffee, Mr. Sporum.

SPORUM

What about a very *small* cup of tea?

KAROLINE

We haven't any tea or coffee.
[*The doorbell rings.*]

SPORUM

The doorbell is ringing, Miss Karoline. It's probably another creditor. All I wish is that the first of the month would never come. Go and see who it is.

KAROLINE

I'm sure it isn't a client.
[*She exits.*]

[66]

SPORUM

[*To himself.*] No tea—no coffee. What a success!

KAROLINE

[*Returns, holding a slip of paper.*] Telephone bill! Final notice—Dr. Max Sporum, attorney at law, is hereby requested, etc., etc. If we don't pay twenty-three marks fifty the phone will be cut off!

SPORUM

Well, we won't pay! The telephone company is crazy! Where would I get twenty-three marks fifty? I couldn't even pay twenty-three pfennigs. Let them cut it off! Throw him out!
[*He sits down.*]

KAROLINE

I *have* thrown him out. [*Adoringly.*] You are nervous today, Mr. Sporum.

SPORUM

Oh, please don't fuss over me.

KAROLINE

I'm not fussing over you. I'm merely stating a fact. [*She puts chair from small table, R. of table, carries a little table to the wall at the right—takes the tray.*]

SPORUM

Then stop stating facts to the effect that I'm nervous. That's a medical diagnosis and you are a law clerk and not a physician!

KAROLINE

Very well, Mr. Sporum.

SPORUM

Oh, all right. Have it your way. I *am* nervous. This first of the month is terrible! All the bills come today. I won't pay a single one, but nevertheless it's terrible! Why do you look at me so significantly? I know I haven't even paid you! But rest assured, you're the only one who will be paid.

KAROLINE

I am greatly honored, Dr. Sporum.
[*She exits with the tray.*]

SPORUM

[*While she is moving about.*] Don't be sarcastic, Miss Karoline. Things are going very badly with me. [KARO-LINE *re-enters.*] I'm afraid you have made a foolish choice. I doubt if there is another lawyer in the whole city who is doing as poorly as I am. I'm so worried that I'm unable to sleep. I read the Bible all night long. It's the only thing that still affords me a little comfort. Those in search of justice have no use for me because I uphold the standard of ethics. What was that phone call a few minutes ago? Who wanted me? Let me see the

[68]

slip. [*Reads.*] Mr. S. Konrad, President of the Argentine Meat Packing and Export Co., Ltd. What does he want?

KAROLINE

His secretary phoned to ask when Mr. Konrad might see you on business. I told him any time.

SPORUM

And that is right, my child. I am upholding the standard of ethics, so I have to starve. Shady cases, I refuse to handle, and the honest ones do not pay. Friends, I have none. Politics, I hate. So here I am, nearly fifty years of age, with all my knowledge and integrity, eking out an existence by scribbling articles for law journals. My practice is nil. How is it going to end? Only one thing is certain . . . it is not going to end by my abandoning the strict standard of ethics. [*Shouting.*] It is not going to end that way, Miss Karoline!

KAROLINE

Don't shout at me as though I wanted you to abandon your precious ethics. I don't! I admire you just because you're willing to endure this poverty!

SPORUM

I'd prefer you to despise me for my wealth! [*Picks up some papers on desk.*] A fine list of cases I have here . . . Sperl vs. Bergman,—the fee won't pay for a pair of shoes. . . . Lehner vs. Greunbaum—at the most that'll pay for a new pair of trousers and short ones at that! My biggest case—Roth vs. Heinitz. . . . I worked on it for two full nights. Yet I'll bet it won't pay for next month's rent. [*Throws documents aside.*] Now look at this desk again. And over there! Everywhere . . . disorder!

KAROLINE

[*Arranging papers.*] But you always throw things around! Now if you had a wife . . .

SPORUM

Yes, that's all I need, isn't it? . . . a family. Well, I'm thankful I haven't got one! There'd be more of us to starve. As it is, I'm the only one to suffer because of my misfortunes, my integrity, my . . . handicaps. [*Looks at the slip again.*] President Konrad—I'm positive that someone is playing a practical joke on me.

KAROLINE

Yes, Dr. Sporum, I thought so too at first, but I called the secretary at his hotel. He said it was about an important legal matter and so I made an appointment for the gentleman to call here at about this time.

SPORUM

Now?

KAROLINE

Yes, Dr. Sporum. He said he'd be here within an hour.

SPORUM

A big business man . . . coming to my shabby office on an important legal matter! Impossible! Those things don't happen! Miss Karoline. [*The doorbell rings. He starts.*] I'll go into the other room, Miss Karoline. You'd better see him first, if it is he.

[*Rushes off stage.* KAROLINE *hurries out and returns a moment later with* LU.]

LU

[*Entering.*] *Good morning.* [*Looks at* KAROLINE.] I wish I were like you. . . . Exactly like you. [*Sighs.*] But I can't be. . . . I can't.

KAROLINE

Excuse me, Madame . . . I don't quite understand.

LU

Don't worry. . . . I'm not crazy. That remark was just a sigh with words. I'm looking for Dr. Max Sporum.

KAROLINE

May I ask your business, Madame?

LU

It's a personal matter. Are you his secretary?

KAROLINE

Yes. Who shall I say is calling?

LU

Mrs. . . . [*She doesn't finish the word.*] Oh, please tell me quickly. . . . Is Dr. Sporum married?

[71]

KAROLINE

No.

LU

[*Relieved.*] Oh, thank Heaven!

KAROLINE

Why? . . . You haven't any designs on the old man, have you?

LU

[*Alarmed.*] Oh, is he old?

KAROLINE

Yes.

LU

I hope he's not *very* old.

KAROLINE

Well—he's much nearer fifty than forty.
　[*She exits L. I.*]

LU

[*Going to front of table. Looks at the desk.*] He *is* poor! I'm sure of that! [SPORUM *enters L. I. He looks pompous and forbidding.* LU *is awed.*] Dr. Sporum?

SPORUM

Yes. Pray be seated, Madame. [LU *sits L. of table.*] What can I do for you?

LU

I want some legal advice.

SPORUM

You said it was a *personal* matter.

LU

It is . . . to me.

SPORUM

Might I ask your name?

LU

I'll tell you later. Won't you let me explain my business first?

SPORUM

If you wish, Madame.

[LU *gives* SPORUM *a furtive look. She is awed again.*]

LU

I'm an unemployed glow-worm.

SPORUM

You're a what?

LU

I show people to their seats in the movies. I glow with my little flashlight in the dark.

SPORUM

I see, a well-known insect. Please go on.

LU

Well, on my day off I went to a thé dansant and met a very wealthy married man. *He took a fancy to me,* but you see, *he just hates immoral women.*

[73]

SPORUM

What of it?

LU

~~But Dr. Sporum, it's very important in this case.~~ He hates tarts, you know and *loose women!* He knows that they're hard to get rid of, and besides an open affair would damage his reputation. He's right, of course, he has the proper 'psychological import' and realizes that the best thing for him is a married woman!

SPORUM

Continue. So far you haven't told me anything.

LU

Well, we danced together, and during the tango I told him a lie, I said I was married to a lawyer. You know, I can always lie more convincingly during a tango.

SPORUM

Go on, please! And I ask you to come to the point! Why have you come to see me?

LU

oh

~~Because~~ I'm frightened! What will happen to me when he finds out that it was a lie? Is it a case of fraud —a crime? What shall I do? [*Weeping.*] I'm prepared to pay well for your legal advice. [*Still weeping, but coquettishly.*] I'll be grateful to you in every way.

[*She makes a coy gesture.*]

[74]

SPORUM

[*Crossing behind her to above table.*] Where is the Bible? [*Searches and finds a big Bible.*]

LU

[*Rises, awed.*] Is there advice for that sort of thing in the Bible?

SPORUM

No, but my glasses are in it! [*Takes gold glasses out, puts them on. Looks at her through them.*] You're a very pretty girl!

LU

Oh yes, I know that. That's why the men run after me.

SPORUM

Oh, do they run after you?

LU

Yes.

SPORUM

Why?

LU

They all want to teach me the facts of life.

SPORUM

And you?

LU

Well, I am very poor, so I have decided to lead an immoral life.

SPORUM

[*Caressing her.*] Poor, pretty, frivolous child.

LU

[*Sinks into his arms. Sitting on edge of table.*] Oh thank you! Thank you! Thank you! [*Sniffs.*] I smell perfume. What is it?

SPORUM

Lily-of-the-valley. But let us get to the point. I have only one question to ask you. Did you accept money or jewels from him under your assumed name?

LU

Under what name?

SPORUM

The name of the lawyer's wife.

LU

Oh, no . . . I never accepted a single penny under any name. All I had was a few teas, a cold supper; flowers. . . .

SPORUM

They don't count. You'd have had them in any case. Well, then . . . [*As though reciting a lesson.*] Your thoughtless procedure whereby you did cunningly and artfully mislead someone into an erroneous belief, but from which you did not derive any unlawful gain, does not fall within the legal interpretation of fraud accord-

ing to the provisions of Section 379 of the Penal Code.
As you gave no name you are innocent of the charge
of impersonation according to Section 143 of the Penal
Code. Thus, my child, from the legal point of view,
you are not guilty of anything. I'm in a position to
completely reassure you on that point.

> [*He pats her. He has been caressing her through-
> out the speech and now makes a bolder gesture.*]

Lu

[*With a sigh.*] Oh, I envy the woman whose fate lies
in the hand of a strong man!

Sporum

Pardon me, but my hand slipped.

Lu

It's this slippery material.

Sporum

Well, don't worry, my child. Be happy that you are
young and pretty. You still have all your life before
you.

Lu

You are so kind-hearted, Mr. Sporum. You give me
courage.

Sporum

Not at all. I am only doing my duty.

[77]

Lu

[*Breaks from his arms, sits down L. of table.* Sporum *sits R. of table.*] Oh, I've just remembered! . . . I forgot to mention something when I told you my story. It's a mere detail and I'm sure it has no importance, legally.

Sporum

What was it?

Lu

Well—this man insisted so much that I finally had to tell him my husband's name.

Sporum

How do you mean?

Lu

The telephone directory happened to be lying on the table, so I opened it at random . . . and chose the name of a lawyer.

Sporum

Excellent! [*Laughs, greatly amused.*] Just on the chance.

Lu

Yes.

Sporum

[*Laughing loudly.*] Excellent! And who was it?

Lu

You.

SPORUM

What!

LU

You.

SPORUM

Me!

LU

Yes. I gave him your name . . . I told him you were my husband.

SPORUM

That I—am your husband?

LU

Yes. That's right . . . Your name was the first on the page—in the top left-hand corner.

SPORUM

In the top left-hand corner!

LU

A while ago you asked me my name. I will tell you now. [*Rises and makes him a bow.*] Mrs. Max Sporum! [*Sits down again.*]

SPORUM

[*Angrily.*] I'll have you jailed for that!

LU

But didn't you just say. . . ?

Sporum

[*Rising.*] This is different! . . . You gave a false name, and you are therefore guilty of impersonation . . . but not according to Section 143 of the Penal Code, because you did not assume a false name in order to deceive a public official. Instead, you cunningly and artfully deceived a private individual, and therefore your offense is far more serious! It comes under Section 379 of the Penal Code. And this cold supper at an expensive hotel cost a great deal of money. It represents something of value received by you. It constitutes an unlawful gain which you obtained by means of a false name. It is fraud, according to the provisions of Section 379 of the Penal Code! The penalty is twelve months in prison or five years in the house of correction. You will go to jail, Madame! You'll serve time for this! [Lu *weeps softly.* Sporum *demands furiously.*] Why did you do it? Were you drunk?

Lu

A little.

Sporum

What made you marry into the telephone book? Why didn't you invent a name?

[*Sits back of table.*]

Lu

I wanted to make someone rich.

Sporum

What is that you say?

Lu

He is looking for a lawyer.

Sporum

Who's looking for a lawyer?

Lu

My friend. He can make you rich with the stroke of his pen.

Sporum

How?

Lu

It's enough to tell you that it means a very large but assured income, and he is willing to give it all to us. By the stroke of his pen he can make some lawyer rich and happy. So why should we miss such a golden opportunity? Why let it vanish in the air like cigarette smoke?

[*She sobs.*]

Sporum

[*Suspecting evil.*] Good Heavens! What's this man's name?

Lu

Konrad.

Sporum

[*Pulls out the slip and reads.*] S. W. Konrad, President. Is that the man?

Lu

Yes . . . yes.

Sporum

And this gentleman wishes to assist your husband as a reward for your . . . your. . . .

Lu

Yes. . . . yes . . . At last you understand.

Sporum

And this gentleman will call on me this morning because you . . . you . . . and he. . . .

Lu

That's it, Dr. Sporum. My, but it takes you a long time to get things.

Sporum

It's unbelievable! How utterly vicious and how fiendishly clever!

Lu

Don't look at me so murderously, you awful man! Why, I thought you'd be pleased!

Sporum

[*Rising, indignantly.*] Do you think everyone is as corrupt as you are? There are still some people who have moral scruples.

Lu

Oh, excuse me, I didn't know that.

[82]

Sporum

How horrible! How perfectly horrible! A monster with a pretty face.

Lu

All right, then . . . If that's the way you feel about it, I'll confess everything and call it all off!

Sporum

[*Furious.*] Don't do that!

Lu

[*Happily.*] Then you accept?

Sporum

Certainly not!

Lu

[*Sadly.*] You don't accept?

Sporum

No . . . that is to say . . . Wait a minute. [*Excitedly.*] It isn't as simple as that. You just wait a minute please! What's the hurry? You just wait a minute, will you? You've placed me in a very awkward position.

Lu

Why? If I were really Mrs. Sporum then you'd have a right to say that, but I'm not.

Sporum

If you were my wife, nothing like this could happen. Wait! I must try to think clearly. Well, let's consider the facts. How horrible. That man will be here almost immediately! He's already made the appointment!

Lu

There, you see, everything I've said is true.

Sporum

What a dreadful blow! It is all so sudden, too. Just a minute, please . . . I'm so upset. . . . My thoughts have scattered to the four winds . . . Oh, it's horrible. [*Shouts, facing her.*] What do you want of me?

Lu

I'm not asking you to take part in any deep dyed plot. All I want you to do is accept. It will give me strength, if someone else's fate depends on it. It will help me to make a decision.

Sporum

What? Then you haven't . . . yet. . . .

Lu

No. But it's been arranged for tonight.

Sporum

How horrible. It's been arranged! What shall I do?

LU

Why ask me, darling?

SPORUM

What? You call *me* darling!

LU

Why not?

SPORUM

[*Blustering.*] Let me see, if you haven't as yet. . . .

LU

And I haven't. . . .

SPORUM

And it's been arranged for?

LU

Tonight.

SPORUM

Horrible! [*Flaring up.*] If you had only held your tongue about how I was to get this contract. *I uphold the standard of ethics, so how can I possibly accept?* [*Despairingly.*] Oh, why did you come here? Why! Why!

LU

Well, when I do a good deed, I hope to get a little something in return . . .

SPORUM

[*Suspiciously.*] Ah-h!

LU

Say, a little gratitude, or a little love from somebody.

[85]

SPORUM

If you'd only come to me afterwards!

LU

I thought of that, too, but if you'd happened to let slip that you weren't married, the whole thing would have fallen through. I have to be businesslike, even though I am a good fairy.

SPORUM

Oh, never mind about your good fairies! You're not a fairy—you're a little goose.

LU

Really? Oh, you make me so happy, darling. That's my ideal.

SPORUM

Why didn't you say you are my daughter?

LU

Oh, go on! Who does anything for a father? And besides, how was I to know that you were old enough to be my father? But it's a good thing you *are* such an old fool, because it seems more likely that I *would* be unfaithful to you . . . right and left.

SPORUM

Right and left?

LU

Yes.

SPORUM

Thanks, awfully. And how did you know that I was poor?

LU

I am a good fairy. I never make mistakes because I never think. Please, dear doctor, don't send me to prison. Don't you see I could have undone everything with a single word? Yet I have come down to earth with a lovely miracle, and I want these dull people on earth to believe in the miracle. Think it over calmly. Let me make you happy. You really deserve it, you dear old idiot, you.

SPORUM

[*Exasperated.*] I object to the tone in which. . . .

LU

Don't you worry about my tone, darling. A little rudeness will do you good, now that you are weakening.

SPORUM

Witch! . . . goose! . . . witch! . . . you're a perfect cross between a witch and a goose!

LU

Oh, it's a good sign when you begin calling me names. Look here, you must be sensible. Konrad will be here any minute. Afterwards I'm going away forever and you'll be happy. . . . Oh, don't be angry. . . . Let's have a little talk. Or shall I go?

SPORUM

Courtesy forbids me to ask you . . . to leave. And, anyway, I know that you wish to stay here till your millionaire arrives so that he will find you with me.

LU

That's right. We might as well be honest about it . . . Although it wasn't so hard to guess, was it, Judge?

SPORUM

I'm not a judge!

LU

No, but you will be, and then you'll laugh.

SPORUM

I won't laugh.

LU

I promise you, you'll be a judge.

SPORUM

I positively will not laugh.

LU

[*After a long pause.*] Isn't this too bad? But it's just like me. Now that I should talk I can't think of anything to talk about!

SPORUM

That's the time to keep quiet.

Lu

All right.
[*Resigns herself. Silence. Looks about her.*]

Sporum

What are you looking for?

Lu

The dog.

Sporum

What dog?

Lu

There's a sign outside that says "Beware of the dog."

Sporum

There is no dog here!

Lu

Than what's the sign for?

Sporum

[*Embarrassed.*] Bill collectors.

Lu

Oh! What's that over there on the wall?

Sporum

A map.

[89]

Lu

What's *that* for?

Sporum

I have to hang *something* on the wall. [*Pause.*] Old masters are too expensive this year.

Lu

[*Pause. With a sigh.*] What's that great big green country over there?

Sporum

Russia!

Lu

What's that little red spot in the upper corner?

Sporum

That, my child, is Europe.

Lu

Thanks.

Sporum

That's all right.

Lu

I've learned something.

Sporum

I'm very glad.
    [*Pause.*]

Lu

I've got a heart but no one in it.

Sporum

[*Bitterly.*] Except me!

Lu

Except you, darling.

Sporum

I'm a fine figure of a man!

Lu

Yes . . . for your age. . . . May I ask an indiscreet question?

Sporum

Please do!

Lu

I know you're not married, but there's some woman in your life, isn't there?

Sporum

[*Nervously.*] Oh . . . I say . . . really. . . .

Lu

Then there isn't a woman?
[*Bell rings.* Karoline *enters from left, crosses room and exits right.* Lu *looks at* Karoline *and back to* Sporum, *meaningly.*]

Lu

Oh, I see. . . . Max, you must make this woman happy!

Sporum

What?

Lu

That girl ought to have a baby by you.

Sporum

What!

Lu

Give her a beautiful baby! It's your duty!

Sporum

My what?

Lu

Your duty! Good gracious, are you deaf? I have to tell you everything twice.

Sporum

I'm *not* deaf! But you are so brazen that I always think I haven't heard you correctly.

Lu

Don't snap, you funny old bear! [*Smile.*] You foundling!

Sporum

Foundling? That's a libel on my parents. I was not a foundling!

Lu

To me you are a foundling, darling, because I found you in the telephone book! Don't be angry. That's nothing to be ashamed of. Moses was a foundling, too, and he became general manager!

Sporum

Tch . . . how perfectly awful!

Lu

[*Imitating him impishly.*] Perfectly awful!

Sporum

[*As though to himself.*] I'll end by killing her, this tactless glow-worm . . . you're a triple cross between a witch, an idiot and a glow-worm.

Lu

Thanks.
[Karoline *enters; stops in the doorway.*]

Sporum

Who was that?

Karoline

A collector . . . for the installment on the books . . . Shakespeare's works.

Sporum

Have you thrown him out?

[93]

KAROLINE

Yes.

[*Leaves left. Little pause.*]

LU

[*Pause.*] Oh "Midsummer Night's Dream" is so beautiful. . . . "Titania" . . . that *should* have been my name . . . or Puck, perhaps. [*Pause.*] I'm much better with music. Without music I can't really be a good fairy.

SPORUM

How are you fairies doing nowadays?

LU

We are dying out!

[*Pause.*]

SPORUM

[*Aside.*] Strange! I'm sitting here with her and I don't kill her! I don't know what's the matter with me! [*Looking at* LU.] Well? What now?

LU

I don't know anything else to talk about. Aren't any more collectors coming?

SPORUM

Oh, certainly!

[*The bell rings.* SPORUM *nods his head to indicate there's another.*]

LU

[*Relieved.*] Oh!
  [KAROLINE *enters; stops in doorway.*]

KAROLINE

A collector from the laundry.

SPORUM

Did you throw him out?

KAROLINE

Yes.
  [KAROLINE *exits.*]

LU

Laundry! I *love laundry!* [*Pause.* SPORUM *stares.*] But then, I need nice undies. [*Pause.*] With me they are always on display. Oh, don't misunderstand me, please! [*Weeping.*] It is one of my greatest sorrows. The first thing they all do is undress me. The painter, the photographer, the tailor, the theatrical manager, the film director, and the doctor. Once I was even undressed by a dentist!

SPORUM

Surely not by force!

LU

Oh no! He just asked me to.

SPORUM

Whereupon you immediately undressed yourself?

[95]

Lu

Why, of course! You see, I always say to myself . . . you know, I *have* a nice little figure . . . so I always say to myself, "Let the poor boys see it. It makes them happy." . . . Would *you* like to see it?

[*Half rising. Lifts her dress coquettishly.*]

Sporum

[*In great consternation.*] No, thank you! No . . . no!

Lu

That's my one passion—doing good, no matter how it has to be done.

Sporum

You ought to go on the stage!

Lu

Oh, no. I don't want to do *too* much good! [*Door bell rings energetically.*] Oooh, that's the President!

Sporum

So you recognize his ring.

Lu

No, that's the first time I've heard it. But I know it's the President.

[KAROLINE *enters excitedly.*]

Karoline

President Konrad is here!

[*96*]

SPORUM

[*Presses his hand to his heart.*] Good God!

LU

[*Rising. Quickly to* KAROLINE.] Let him come in, Miss.

SPORUM

[*Nervously.*] Wait, Miss Karoline.
  [*Buries his head in his hands, in a panic of inde-
    cision.*]

KAROLINE

I can't keep him waiting. Shall I let him come in or not?

LU

[*To* SPORUM *in a whisper.*] Let him in. You'll see. He'll act as though he didn't know me. He's going to lie like anything. He is a *real* gentleman! [SPORUM *nods affirmatively to* KAROLINE. *Grips the table.* KARO-LINE *exits happily. To* SPORUM.] What's the matter with you?

SPORUM

I'm going to faint in a minute. I'm not used to all this excitement.
  [KAROLINE *shows* KONRAD *in and exits.*]

KONRAD

My name is S. W. Konrad.

[97]

SPORUM

[*Rising and crossing to* KONRAD *shaking hands, and starts back.*] I am Dr. Sporum.

KONRAD

Won't you introduce me to the charming lady?

SPORUM

[*Stammering.*] As a matter of fact she is . . . is . . . [KONRAD *kissing hand to* LU.]

LU

[*Interrupts.*] Why, Max! Aren't you going to introduce the President?

[*Almost fainting with excitement,* MAX *points to* KONRAD *and then to* LU.]

KONRAD

[*Steps forward and kisses her hand.*] President Konrad.

LU

[SPORUM *tries to stop her from offering refreshments.*] I am pleased to meet you, President. Won't you sit down? May I get you a cup of coffee or perhaps you'd prefer tea?

KONRAD

Thank you, Madame. Neither. Well, may I come to the point at once?

SPORUM

[*Uneasily.*] As far as I'm concerned, I'd like to say . . .

Lu

[*Interrupting*. KONRAD *kisses hand to* LU.] But Max . . . [*To* KONRAD.] Please go on, Mr. President.

KONRAD

Well, my dear Dr. Sporum. I wish to appoint you as the legal representative for Central Europe of my firm, the Argentine Meat Packing and Export Co., Ltd.

Lu

Bravo! This month is starting off beautifully! But, Maxie, didn't I predict it this morning . . . in bed?
[SPORUM *darts her an angry look.*]

KONRAD

We can leave the details for another time. To be brief, we have an immense number of contracts and countless small law-suits, all simple work but a lot of it. Your income would be very considerable.

Lu

How lovely! That's what we've always dreamed of . . . in bed.
[*Another angry look from* SPORUM.]

KONRAD

Later on, when we are accustomed to working together, there will be larger cases. But for the present I have come here only to learn whether or not you accept.

[99]

SPORUM

And, may I ask, sir, why you come to me?

KONRAD

[*Blows kiss to* LU, *secretly.*] The Embassy recommended you. Mmm . . . there seems to be a strong odor of lily-of-the-valley here.

SPORUM

That's me, sir. Won't you go on?

KONRAD

Very well. All the particulars which will be of interest to you are contained in a document which I will send you. So that for now that's all I've got to say.

SPORUM

Are you *sure* that I was recommended by your Embassy?

KONRAD

What do you mean by that, Mr. Sporum?

LU

But Maxie, the President is not a fool!
[SPORUM *looks at* LU.]

KONRAD

I've become quite a stranger here. That's why I turned to them for advice. You see, we've got law suits,

KAROLINE

No.

SPORUM

Credit?

KAROLINE

Of course.

SPORUM

Let's leave it there for the present. I'm terribly nervous. I'll have a good look at it later on and decide then where it belongs. *What are these things?*

KAROLINE

This is the new filing cabinet, the latest model, it's fireproof. This . . . is an adding machine, and this . . . a new typewriter.
[*Phone.*]

SPORUM

Hello? What? The Chrysler Company? Just a minute, please—— [*To* KAROLINE.] Somebody wants to demonstrate a car for me! What does it mean? Is that some more of your work?

KAROLINE

Yes. That's Order 24. A little Chrysler—on easy payments!

SPORUM

Hello! [*Into phone.*] Well, I'll have a look at it! But without any obligation on my part, of course! Very well—— Yes! Tomorrow morning would be convenient,

[125]

but I'm a very busy man, you know! Right! [*Hangs up receiver.*] Aren't you over-stepping the mark, Miss Karoline?

KAROLINE

Oh, now really—Dr. Sporum—it's only a little four-seater! Why, every lawyer has one!

SPORUM

A four-passenger! Oh, Karoline—what a difference between yesterday and today.

KAROLINE

Oh, please—don't remind me!
[*Takes up a paper.*]

SPORUM

What is that, Miss Karoline?

KAROLINE

Notes. May I report?

SPORUM

Certainly.

KAROLINE

[*Pointing to a document.*] This is a contract, which the President signed.

SPORUM

When did he sign it?

[126]

KAROLINE

Last night—at exactly half past nine—in his shirt-sleeves!

SPORUM

[*Startled*.] What do you mean—shirt-sleeves?

KAROLINE

He was just about to put on his coat. It was half past nine!

SPORUM

Are you *sure*?

KAROLINE

Of course, Mr. Sporum. I looked at my watch.

SPORUM

Very well. And what is this other paper?

KAROLINE

This is the company's plan of operation—drawn up by the legal department! [*Picks up another paper*.] And this—is the result of a little figuring I did last night! I couldn't sleep—so I made an estimate of our probable monthly income! We'll be able to meet all current expenses and bank an average of 10,000 per month! In twelve months, that makes——

SPORUM

One hundred and twenty thousand—and in a hundred years—twelve millions! Pretty nice, eh? More than I'd hoped for!

[127]

KAROLINE

God bless the Embassy!

SPORUM

Dear God! I can't realize it, Miss Karoline! Is it a vision or a dream? I couldn't sleep all night. [*Changes his tone abruptly.*] Thank you, Miss Karoline—you may go now! [KAROLINE *exits.* SPORUM *to himself.*] *Am I a scoundrel? No—not legally! But I'm no longer the paragon I was yesterday!* [*Rises. Glances up at the wall.*] It's very beautiful—that picture there! *I'm going to buy it!* [*Enjoys repeating the words differently.*] I'm going to buy *it! I'm* going to buy! I'm going to buy a picture! I *like* it and therefore—*I'm going to buy it! Why not?*—what *am* I doing? *Talking out loud in an empty room like a radio?* I'm *reciting a monologue! What's come over me? Am I crazy?* [*The phone rings.* KAROLINE *enters, carrying a new, bright yellow brief case.*] Hello? Yes, of course! *Now!* Yes, half past four—Certainly! Any time! I shall be in all afternoon. I'll be delighted to see him! Goodbye! [*Hangs up phone. To* KAROLINE.] Mr. Konrad's secretary! Mr. Konrad is coming here!

KAROLINE

[*Excitedly.*] When?

SPORUM

He's just leaving. He'll be here in half an hour—and *of course—everything is upside down!*

KAROLINE

All the better! He'll be impressed—[*Almost shouting with joy.*]—with the activity—preparation—organization——

SPORUM

Steady, steady! Calm yourself, Miss Karoline! What have you there?

KAROLINE

A gorgeous, new pig-skin brief case. Order No. 29. [*Puts it on his desk.*]

SPORUM

Oh, that's a beauty! And we must also prepare for our guest! Have we any cognac, cigarettes, cigars? We must offer him something, you know.

KAROLINE

I'll get them immediately! They'll bring the total number of orders to 51! [*Goes to main entrance.* CLERK *brings in packages.*] Give them to me, please!
 [*Takes packages.* CLERK *exits.*]

SPORUM

What are those?

KAROLINE

[*Hurriedly placing packages on desk.*] Orders 46 and 47! Six boxes of pencils—a pencil-sharpener—1,000 paper clips—and this thing here—is a stapling machine.
 [*Rushes out.*]

[129]

SPORUM

Ah! *A pencil-sharpener!* [*Begins trying it out.*] The dream of my childhood! How I longed for one as a boy! And now—at *last*—I've got it! I've got it!
[*Unpacking the machine.*]

KAROLINE

[*Returns.*] The lady is here.

SPORUM

What lady?

KAROLINE

Yesterday's! The *crazy one!*
[*Enter* LU. KAROLINE *exits.*]

LU

Good morning.

SPORUM

Hello. What does *this* mean? *Yesterday* you said "*good-bye*" forever—and *now you're here again!*

LU

Yes, what have you got there?

SPORUM

A pencil sharpener! Look at it! *The dream of my childhood!* The *dearest wish of Sporum*—the *boy! I've waited for it*—for *forty years!*

[130]

Lu

And what are all these packages?

Sporum

[*Gleefully.*] *Preparation! Organization! Equipment!*
Do have a seat!

Lu

Thank you. [*Sits down and heaves a great sigh.*] Ah,
my friend——

Sporum

What a deep sigh! [*Sympathetically.*] My poor, pretty
child—I can guess what it means.

Lu

Oh—*what* a *night!*
[*Wipes away a few tears.*]

Sporum

*Poor little thing! It must have been perfectly awful!
But at any rate—it's all over now! You've done it—so
it's done with.*

Lu

Yes, I've done it——

Sporum

Poor child.

Lu

Don't pity me, please! I'm *not unhappy!*

[131]

SPORUM

[*Sarcastically.*] Ah! You're *happy!*

LU

We don't look at it quite the same way. There's just a little difference. [*Look from* SPORUM.] I don't think it's of the *least* importance—legally.

SPORUM

And what *is* this difference?

LU

I—I've *done* it—but—*not with him!*

SPORUM

Not with him?

LU

No. With someone *else!*

SPORUM

But at *ten o'clock last night*——

LU

I didn't keep the appointment!

SPORUM

Then what *did* you do?

Lu

I didn't go till eleven—and then—*not to him,* but—to *someone else!* What did you say these packages were?

Sporum

Preparation! Organization! Equipment!

Lu

Didn't you get too much?

Sporum

We needed a good many things.

Lu

I'm afraid,—*you won't need that many. You won't have so much to do after all! I'm afraid you won't have anything to do!*

Sporum

Why? What's happened?

Lu

He caught me!
[*There falls a long pause.* Karoline *enters.*]

Karoline

[*In a low voice.*] Excuse me, but the man is getting impatient about the picture!

[133]

SPORUM

Wait—my child! The fate of the picture is just being *decided!* I'll let you know in a few moments! [KARO-LINE *exits.*] Well—*so he caught you,* eh?

LU

Yes! *He caught me——*

SPORUM

Isn't it funny? Now—I don't know what to ask you next?

LU

You should ask me with *whom* he caught me!

SPORUM

Well—with whom did he catch you?

LU

With—*someone else!*

SPORUM

[*Angrily.*] A charming answer, that!—I'm so confused! I don't understand at all——

LU

Unfortunately, it's *very simple! I couldn't sell my-self for money!* I made a last try—but I *couldn't!* So that's *that!* Now, I'll *never* try again! I'm *happy*—it's only *you*—I'm *sorry for——!*

[134]

SPORUM

[*Rings the bell.* KAROLINE *enters on left. She leaves the door open behind her.*] We don't want the picture, Karoline!

> [KAROLINE *beckons through door.* MAN *enters and removes picture; out with* KAROLINE. LU *and* SPORUM *look blankly to front during this.*]

LU

Yesterday . . . I kept hoping I could . . . until the evening. At ten o'clock . . . it still seemed quite likely . . . that we'd both be rich. Then at eleven . . . I decided. . . . For a moment I thought of you intensely . . . but I couldn't. I felt sure you wouldn't have expected it of me.

SPORUM

God forbid!

LU

I knew you wouldn't!

SPORUM

And so you decided all by yourself——

LU

What difference does that make?

SPORUM

Well—did someone help you to decide?

[135]

Lu

Yes—someone did—at the last moment!

Sporum

Who was it?

Lu

The other one!

Sporum

[*Explosively.*] And you listened to such a scoundrel?

Lu

Scoundrel?

Sporum

[*Shouting.*] Do you mean to say that—this unscrupulous blackguard—this unspeakable cad—exercised more influence over you, than the voice of your own convictions? You—you little idiot?

Lu

Look here! Why are you calling me names?

Sporum

I'm not calling you names! I'm talking about this man! On my honor—I don't know what I'm talking about!

[*Sits down very suddenly.*]

Lu

[*Trying to comfort him.*] Come—be nice to me, darling, won't you? [*Points to wall.*] Look! The map is much prettier than the picture! It's nice and bright! There's imagination in it!

SPORUM

Yes—— [*To himself, meditatively.*] What a scoundrel!

[*Pause.*]

LU

We're sitting here just like yesterday—when we were waiting for him!

SPORUM

[*Bitterly.*] There's just a little difference.

LU

Which, however . . .

SPORUM

[*Scathingly.*] Is not of the least importance . . . legally, I know! [*He bursts out suddenly*.] It all came so suddenly. . . . And now this awful change. Oh, forgive me.

LU

Go ahead! Please shout—if it relieves you!

SPORUM

[*Shouts.*] Why, oh why—did all this have to happen?

LU

Because we cheated him!

[137]

SPORUM

We?

LU

Well, I did! Or rather—I didn't cheat him—I merely failed to keep my part of the bargain!

SPORUM

And—subsequently, made your offense even more serious by——

LU

——Keeping the bargain with someone else!

SPORUM

And—further aggravated the situation—by allowing him to——

LU

——Catch me!

SPORUM

Full stop! That will do—I haven't had a case as clearly stated in this office for years! [*Forlornly.*] Good-bye—packages—machines, clips—and envelopes! [*Rings bell.* KAROLINE *enters immediately. She stops in the doorway.*] Karoline—all the packages must be returned.

KAROLINE

Good heavens!

SPORUM

Karoline! One of your best qualities . . . is that you never ask questions.

[KAROLINE *tries to speak.*]

[138]

SPORUM

In this instance—I must particularly request you not to.

KAROLINE

Very well, Dr. Sporum. I'll make the necessary arrangements at once! We've received 51 items—— Now, I'll have to count backwards!

SPORUM

[*As she is about to exit.*] Karoline—there is a tear in your eye!

KAROLINE

[*Heroically.*] Two, Mr. Sporum—two!
  [*Exits.*]

SPORUM

What a pity! As a matter of fact—well, let's be honest about it—it was beastly of me! But I'd explained it away so brilliantly to my own conscience! It was one of my best legal efforts!

LU

A legal mind must be a great comfort.

SPORUM

It's a strange thing—it isn't the picture that I mind losing. It's the pencil sharpener. [LU *nods,* SPORUM *hangs his head. Long pause.*] I don't suppose he'll forgive you?

[139]

Lu

That's out of the question.

Sporum

It must have been a great disappointment to Konrad.

Lu

Yes.

Sporum

But he didn't have any claims on you—

Lu

No claims—but hopes—and they hurt more——

Karoline

[*Entering.*] President Konrad is here.

Lu

[*Running to door at left.*] I'm not here—and I haven't been here!
　　[*Exits.*]

Sporum

[*To* Karoline.] Show him in. [Karoline *exits and returns with* Konrad. Sporum *rises, receives* Konrad *with great dignity.*] This is an honor, President. Will you have something to drink? Cognac, cigars, cigarettes? Please have a seat—here! You're looking very well, indeed——

[140]

KONRAD

I'm surprised to hear that, Dr. Sporum! I had a very bad night! What are all these packages?

SPORUM

Preparation! Organization! Equipment!

KONRAD

I see, well, well, . . . may I . . .

SPORUM

Oh! please, Mr. President——
  [*Indicates* KONRAD *to sit.*]

KONRAD

Are we alone?

SPORUM

[*Rings bell. Through door.*] Karoline? [KAROLINE *appears.*] We are not to be disturbed, Miss Karoline. [KAROLINE *nods and exits.*] *Well,* sir?

KONRAD

[*Sits L. of table.*] Can anyone hear me?

SPORUM

Oh, no.

KONRAD

No danger of eavesdropping?

SPORUM

Oh, never! You—you alarm me!

KONRAD

I'm afraid I'll have to!

SPORUM

For God's sake—has anything happened?

KONRAD

[*Wryly.*] It has!—please listen!

SPORUM

Yes, sir! Well——

KONRAD

You'll be surprised to hear what I'm about to say, but in the end, you'll realize that I was forced to tell you everything—no matter how unusual it may be!

SPORUM

I am listening, sir!

KONRAD

Last night I got into my car outside of the hotel——

SPORUM

At what time?

KONRAD

At eleven! I had a—an—appointment at ten—— [*Look between them.*] —but it had been previously cancelled!—So, as I've said—at eleven o'clock, I got into my car outside the hotel! Not at the main entrance, but at the side entrance, where the private cars are parked. As a matter of fact—it was in front of the service entrance! Please note that: because it's very important—*the service entrance*. Just ahead of my car was a taxi. We both started at exactly the same time, but as the taxi was trying to pull out of the row of cars, it suddenly backed—without warning—collided with us and smashed my brand new Zeiss headlamps! The lamps had only been fitted to the car the day before. They had been made especially for me at the factory and cost a small fortune! Almost as much as some cars! Well, the taxi smashed them for me and then proceeded to drive off—without paying any attention whatever! I was so furious, that I said to my chauffeur: "Albert, follow that taxi and catch up with it—even if it takes till tomorrow morning!" You see, my car is insured against damage, but the lamps mentioned in the policy, were two cheap lamps, which I had replaced with the more expensive ones, so that I didn't know whether or not the Insurance Company would have to make good my loss! [*Nod from* SPORUM.] Well, we chased the taxi all over the city—never losing sight of it for a moment! At last, it stopped in front of a house! It stopped—and who do you think got out of it? Hold tight, Dr. Sporum—the headwaiter at my hotel—and —your charming wife, Mrs. Max Sporum! [SPORUM *remains calm and motionless*.] The head waiter paid the driver, offered his arm to Mrs. Sporum and led her into the house—where, I later learned—he lives! [*Pause*.] —*the waiter!* [SPORUM *still sits motionless*.] I was so

[143]

amazed that I decided to wait! I waited to see when your wife would come out! Well, sir—for your information—they went in at ten minutes past eleven—and it was exactly half past two—when they came out again! [SPORUM *shows no sign of emotion whatever.*] Your wife then took a taxi and drove off, but not before she and the waiter had exchanged a long, lingering kiss —which lasted so long . . . that it made me sick to watch it! [KONRAD *pauses, leans back . . . then leans forward to* SPORUM.] Well, sir, *what do you say to that?*

SPORUM

[*With decision.*] The case is clear—! The Insurance Company *must* pay for the lamps!

KONRAD

[*Jumps to his feet.*] What? Is that all you have to say?

SPORUM

Yes. The theory of the "navis refecta,"——

KONRAD

What?

SPORUM

—or—"the renovated ship"—was already known in Roman law. If in the course of time, every individual part of a ship were replaced by a new part—the vessel, nevertheless, remained one and the same legal entity! The Insurance on your car, therefore—includes all the fittings!

[144]

KONRAD

[*Derisively.*] Magnificent! And have you nothing to say to your wife's spending the night with a waiter?

SPORUM

With a waiter?

KONRAD

[*Contemptuously.*] Well, a head waiter, if that makes any difference.

SPORUM

Please don't get excited! You must forgive me if I have only considered the *legal* aspect. Force of habit, you know . . . but now I'm beginning to understand. So the lady spent quite a time with the head waiter?

KONRAD

[*Sits left of table.*] Quite a time.

SPORUM

And you waited in the street until dawn?

KONRAD

Yes.

SPORUM

In other words . . . you were spying on her?

KONRAD

What does this mean? Are you angry with me?

[145]

SPORUM

No. I'm not angry with you, but it seems *rather odd* that you should sit in your car . . . from eleven to half past two, when it had nothing to do with you. What concern was it of yours?

KONRAD

I say! I'm really amazed! I admire you, Dr. Sporum! You've got nerves of steel!

SPORUM

Let's stick to the point! Will you kindly answer a few questions?

KONRAD

Certainly! Fire ahead!

SPORUM

[*As though cross-examining.*] You saw the features of the lady under discussion, quite clearly?

KONRAD

Distinctly.

SPORUM

Did she wear a veil?

KONRAD

No.

SPORUM

Wasn't it dark?

[146]

KONRAD

She was standing under a street lamp.

SPORUM

Aren't you near-sighted?

KONRAD

No, I'm far-sighted.

SPORUM

I must point out that you had only seen the lady once in your life—that was yesterday—here in this office—and then for a very short time! How is it possible—that you were able to recognize her—in a fraction of a second—on an exceedingly dark night?

KONRAD

[*Excited.*] I beg your pardon, but you are examining me, as though I were the defendant! I'm not! I'm the plaintiff!

SPORUM

I beg your pardon, but the plaintiff must prove his case!

KONRAD

[*Mockingly.*] I think I understand you, sir! You're the typical husband! You're building me a bridge, over which I may retreat—but retreat is out of the question! I have not told you all! There is something else which makes retreat impossible and—proves my case—as well.

[147]

SPORUM

Well?

KONRAD

I spoke to Mrs. Sporum.

SPORUM

When she went in—or when she came out?

KONRAD

When she came out!

SPORUM

And what did you say to her?

KONRAD

I said: "Madame, I've seen what I've seen and I warn you that there will be consequences!"

SPORUM

And what did she say to that?

KONRAD

She said, "You bet." And then she boxed my ears. [*They catch each other's eye.*] She boxed my ears in the presence of the waiter and my chauffeur. It struck me like a blow in the face.

SPORUM

[*Calmly.*] She was quite right!

[148]

KONRAD

[*Rises.*] WHAT?

SPORUM

Why did you spy on her?

KONRAD

[*Furiously.*] I was trying to get the taxi's number! I had to have it!

SPORUM

But you didn't have to have it, because the Insurance Company has got to pay you! I've just told you so!

KONRAD

[*Pushing chair near table.*] But I hadn't talked to you then——

SPORUM

Why didn't you come to me first?

KONRAD

Because, you might have said that the Insurance Company didn't have to pay and I might never have found the taxi!

SPORUM

No, but then—you wouldn't have had your ears boxed! That's logic, Mr. President! That's logic!

KONRAD

[*Crossing to R. of table. Glares at* SPORUM *a minute.*] Well, we won't discuss the matter any further, Dr.

[149]

Sporum. The fact is that your wife has boxed my ears in the presence of two witnesses! I'm not going to take her to Court—nor am I going to demand satisfaction from you, but you must realize, that under the circumstances, we cannot continue our relations—— Either business or social! I, therefore, trust that you will deem it quite natural, if I avail myself of the cancellation clause, in our contract—and terminate it forthwith.

SPORUM

[*Gasps.*] Terminate—contract—forthwith——
 [*Faints.* KONRAD *rings.* KAROLINE *enters.*]

KONRAD

[*Ironically.*] Dr. Sporum has fainted—as usual!
 [KAROLINE *gives him some water.* SPORUM *recovers. Exit* KAROLINE.]

SPORUM

I beg your pardon!

KONRAD

I'm amazed at you! Now—you faint! But a little while ago, when I proved to you that your wife had— you sat there like a—a—as if it didn't concern you at all!

SPORUM

That was because you gave me the impression of a jilted lover, who wanted to revenge himself on a lady.

[150]

KONRAD

Dr. Sporum! Do you know what impression you give me? [*Shaking a finger at him.*] Dr. Sporum!—Dr. Sporum!

SPORUM

Well?—Well?

KONRAD

You—you impress me as a husband who views his wife's infidelity with remarkable tolerance!

SPORUM

What do you mean by that?

KONRAD

"THAT! . . . you've guessed the very word! That's what I mean!

SPORUM

[*Shouts. Rises.*] Sir!

KONRAD

I'm beginning to see how wise I was in breaking off our business relations!

SPORUM

[*Calmly.*] Look here, Mr. President, you're a practical man. You came here yesterday intending to make me your legal representative—today you've withdrawn your offer, so further discussion is useless. Now then

. . . you get out of here and get out as quickly as possible . . . for if you are *not* quick about it . . . I'll land you a kick in the traditional place . . . and with both feet at once! *That kick is a specialty of mine!*

KONRAD

I shan't give you the chance, Dr. Sporum.
[*Starts for the door. Enter* Lu.]

LU

Ah, Mr. President? You, here?

KONRAD

[*Close to the door.*] I am just leaving, Madame!

LU

When are we to have the pleasure of seeing you again?

KONRAD

Well—I—not in the very near future!

LU

Well—you wouldn't find me here in any case! There's no need to make a secret of it to such a good client, is there? [*Turns to* KONRAD.] We're going to get a divorce!

KONRAD

Is that so?

[152]

LU

Yes! We're going to get a divorce—a perfectly friendly divorce! Baby has been so kind and noble and now he'll be all alone!

KONRAD

Oh, so baby will be all alone, eh? And you?

LU

I'll probably marry again! A distinguished restaurant proprietor. It would be very nice if you would——

KONRAD

[*Furiously.*] If I became a customer?

LU

Yes! And if you would recommend the restaurant to a few of the better class Bank Presidents! It would be so kind of you—if you'd give my future husband a lift!

KONRAD

Of course, Madame! I'd be *delighted!*

LU

My future husband deserves it!

KONRAD

Oh, that's quite irrelevant!
[*Pause.*]

[153]

Lu

Will you take a liqueur?

Konrad

No, thanks. I'll take my leave—Good-bye, Madame! [*To* Sporum.] Good-bye—BABY!

    [Sporum *makes as though to kick him.* Konrad
      rushes out.]

Lu

[*To* Sporum.] Tell me, darling—what does "irrelevant" mean?

Sporum

It means beside the point!

Lu

[*Relieved.*] Oh, thanks!

Sporum

You little devil! Look at the situation you've placed me in.

Lu

Oh, forgive me, Dr. Sporum—but it was a very simple situation! [*Rapidly.*] First, he had to act as though I didn't know that you knew! I had to act as though I didn't know that you knew it from him! And you had to act as though—you didn't know that I knew that you knew! That's simple . . .

Sporum

Awfully simple.

[154]

Lu

And *irrelevant!*

Sporum

Ah, I feel so relieved! What joy—the nightmare is over.

Lu

Are you happy, darling? As happy as I?

Sporum

Yes, I *am* happy! I'm *really happy!*

Lu

And you've got me to thank for it again!

Sporum

Yes—again! I do thank you, my child! I'm no longer a scoundrel!—I'm pure again. [*To* Karoline, *who comes in and goes up to sofa.*] What's happening about the packages?

Karoline

They're being returned, just as you said! I've been counting backwards! There were fifty-one and now there are only twenty-six! Twenty-five!

Sporum

All right, Karoline! It was only a dream!

Karoline

A dream?

[155]

Sporum

Yes! And now we're coming back to reality again! Back to a clear conscience—moral integrity and its natural consequences, beer and pickled pork. [Karoline *gets brief case from table.*] Are you returning the brief case as well? [Karoline *nods. He takes brief case.*] Thank heaven! It was too beautiful!—Farewell, fickle blonde! Farewell!

[*Gives brief case back to* Karoline.]
[Karoline *exits with brief case.*]

Lu

Well, I'm going too—I'll only stay until the head waiter calls for me. I asked him to come here, so's I could introduce him to you!

Sporum

That was very thoughtful of you! Thanks!

Lu

What's the matter, darling? Will seeing the waiter hurt you?

Sporum

Well—you know, my child—when I come to think of it——

Lu

[*Gently and ecstatically.*] Max! A fairy belongs to the whole world! To people—to animals—to flowers—to waiters——

[*Pause.*]

[156]

SPORUM

Listen, dear child—I'd like to say something that will surprise you!

LU

Well?

SPORUM

Now—I'd like you—to kiss me!

LU

Kiss you?

SPORUM

[*Embarrassed.*] Yes.

LU

Passionately?

SPORUM

Well—yes! Please, kiss me passionately.

LU

That's interesting! Yesterday—you didn't want to!

SPORUM

That was different! Now, there are no moral obstacles!

LU

Oh yes, there are, Maxie! Brand new ones.

SPORUM

What new ones? [*Enter* KAROLINE.] Have you?

[157]

KAROLINE

No—it wasn't a collector—it was a gentleman—he is calling for the lady.

LU

Show him in! [*Enter* WAITER. *Coming to* LU.] Here he is—the new moral obstacle!
[*Exit* KAROLINE.]

SPORUM

Oh, so you are the waiter in question?

LU

Yes! Let me introduce you. Dr. Sporum—the Scoundrel!

SPORUM

Happy to meet you.

LU

He's my fiancé! I'm going to marry him!

SPORUM

Why?

LU

Because he wants to marry me! The only man a girl should have—is the man who wants to marry her!

SPORUM

That sounds convincing!

[158]

WAITER

Dr. Sporum—it was my duty—to interfere—last night! It wasn't that we didn't think of you—we did! Lu cried. She said: "Now Dr. Sporum will have to starve again!"

SPORUM

And what did you say?

WAITER

I said: "What of it?"

SPORUM

[*Shaking him by the hand.*] Very considerate.

WAITER

Forgive me, but I didn't feel that we owed you anything!

LU

But *I* do! [*To* WAITER.] Now that I've introduced you—wait outside. I have a last request to make of Dr. Sporum!

[WAITER *exits.*]

SPORUM

Well, my child?

LU

[*Comes close to him.*] I want to ask you, darling—it's like this! My fiancé is opening a small restaurant—I want you to——

[159]

SPORUM

Eat there?

LU

Oh, no, I needn't ask you that! That goes without saying! We're going to have very distinguished customers—bankers, presidents—Ministers—etc., I want to ask you to do something else for me! You see—there are so many legal difficulties when you buy a restaurant! Contracts—transfers—taxes—fees—commissions —and lawyers are so expensive! Won't you attend to all that for my fiancé?

SPORUM

For nothing?

LU

Yes. For nothing! All right?

SPORUM

All right.

LU

You know—I never can ask anything for myself——

SPORUM

Yes, I know.

LU

But to help others is my specialty. Now, I'm his— good fairy! You'll do it, won't you?

SPORUM

Certainly. With pleasure!

[160]

Lu

And—for nothing?

Sporum

Yes—for nothing!

Lu

[*Rising.*] Come there to eat—we'll give you a good meal!

Sporum

For *nothing?*

Lu

Oh, *no!* Not for nothing—but a *little cheaper!* [Lu *leans over his left shoulder.*] Come and have a look at the place! Make a note of the address: 427 Elisabeth-strasse! Restaurant of the Good Fairy!

[*She walks away from the table.*]

Sporum

Yes. I'll make a note of it. [*Turns on desk lamp. Picks up a pencil and fits it into the pencil-sharpening machine. He sharpens the pencil very, very slowly.*] Just a moment, please—I want to sharpen my pencil—with this—before—they take it away——

> [*To see more clearly, he adjusts the lamp. The light illumines his face. He goes on talking in a low voice, while he slowly turns the handle.*]

Lu

[*In the meantime, she has tiptoed to the door. The room darkens very gradually. She whispers softly as she*

[161]

creeps out.] Four—hundred—and—twenty-seven—
Elisabethstrasse—Restaurant of the Good Fairy.

SPORUM

[*Doesn't realize that she has departed. He continues
to speak softly, as he turns the handle of the machine.*]
I am sharpening—my pencil—for the first—and last
time—with this—lovely—pencil sharpener——
    [*Stage darkens, as the*

CURTAIN FALLS

THE GOOD FAIRY

EPILOGUE

EPILOGUE

The MANAGER *steps before the curtain.*
Please don't go, ladies and gentlemen. With your kind
permission, I have a little experiment to try for you
tonight.

> [*He recollects himself.*]

Forgive me. I should have introduced myself. I am the
producer of this play.

> [*He smiles nervously.*]

I tell you that so that you won't mistake me for an
actor. One has to make these distinctions nowadays,
hasn't one?

> [*He takes the audience more into his confi-*
> *dence.*]

Now about the experiment. I thought I should take
advantage of this moment of silence. . . .

> [*Sounds of scene shifting back stage distract*
> *him.*]

This moment of SILENCE! . . .

> [*Silence back stage. Another apologetic smile.*]

While the scenery is being shifted. . . . Yes. . . .
Well, as I was saying, you may think you've seen the
end of this play, but you're wrong! That wasn't an
ending. Why, when I read the manuscript, I sat down
at once and wrote to the author, Mr. Molnar. "My
dear friend," I said, "isn't it about time that you
authors learned that audiences insist on endings that ARE

endings? You simply can't leave your characters up in the air the way you've done in this play. The Public wants to know what really becomes of characters!"

> [*His indignation changes to the confidential tone.*]

Incidentally, I HOPE we managers know what the public wants. I mean to say, where would we managers be if we didn't know? A lot of our plays would fail!

> [*He draws a letter from his pocket and opens it.*]

Well, Mr. Molnar wrote a most gracious reply to my letter. I'll read you what he wrote.

> [*Reading.*]

"My dear Gilbert," he says, "you are absolutely right."

> [*He looks more closely as though spelling out the words; then explains to the audience:*]

You'll forgive me hesitating. It's . . . it's the Hungarian.

> [*He continues.*]

"We authors have fallen into the bad habit of ending our plays with the final curtain, which, of course, is no ending at all, since every story goes on for ages. Of course, you realize that your suggestion makes the dramatist's work very much harder. However, I find your argument so convincing that I enclose a little scene I have written especially for your theatre, and which you will be good enough to have performed after the play, so that the audience may gaze for a moment into the future lives of the characters whose acquaintance they have made. Your old friend,

Ferencs."

[*He looks up.*]

That's all. And that's the experiment we're trying to-night. Now, if you'll be good enough to sit where you are for 10 years more . . . 10 years, yes; we'll show you what really became of the characters in this fairy tale. Of course, most of the 10 years have passed while I've been speaking. That is, if the actors have changed their clothes, they have.

[*He turns to speak off stage.*]

Everything ready?

[*He is satisfied.*]

All right. Go ahead.

[*To audience.*]

The 10 years have passed. Now you'll see!

LET THE CURTAIN RISE!

[*The* MANAGER *bows and retires behind the curtain. The theatre is slowly darkened. It is pitch black when the curtain rises. The scene is in the same private dining room as in Act I. In the center, is a richly decorated table. Six places have been set. A large basket of flowers is on a chair. At first, nothing is visible. Only* LU's *voice is heard. She is chatting merrily with* KAROLINE.]

LU

[*Walking about table.*] It's sweet of you to help me, darling! You know, darling—I simply adore beautifully appointed tables!

[*The lights go up slowly.* LU *is busy arranging the table decorations. She arranges things and walks*

[167]

to and fro feverishly. Finally, she joins KARO-
LINE *at table.* LU *has not changed, but* KARO-
LINE *has stoutened. They are both in evening
dress. The men who will enter will also be in
evening dress. They all look slightly aged and
are getting grey.* KAROLINE *is walking around
table.*]

LU

You know, darling, I don't like to rely on others.
I'd rather do everything myself. Everything myself——
[*Lights go up completely.*] Doesn't the table look gay,
darling?

KAROLINE

It's really lovely.

LU

[*Looking table over.*] Now come and help me scatter
the flowers sort of—carelessly! [KAROLINE *helps.*] You
know, dear, I like cut flowers strewn about far better
than the conventional bunches in the middle! [*Takes
flowers out of bowl . . .* KAROLINE *takes bowl to serving table. They arrange flowers.*] But I can't deny that
I'm excited! It's touching, somehow, to think that I've
lived to see the tenth anniversary of my marriage!

KAROLINE

And how young you've kept, dear——

LU

That's because I'm happy and I've got my husband
to thank for that! He's a perfect husband! Good gra-

cious! *Ten years——* Ten years today—we've been married!

KAROLINE

How time flies——

LU

Yes. Time flies . . . Put a few more flowers over there. You know, dear . . . I chose this dining room for our anniversary dinner because I've so many memories of the only other evening I spent here . . . ten years ago. It was here that all our fates were decided. Put a few more flowers over there, too, darling. Not so many flowers there. That's too many. [KAROLINE *puts flowers around table during all this.*] It'll be strange to dine here with my guests. Please put the place cards on the glasses. It's incredible. I invited them for eight o'clock and not one of them is here yet. Everyone is late, except you. And what do you think of my husband's being late, too? He ought to be the first to arrive. It's awful for a husband to be late on his tenth wedding anniversary.

KAROLINE

The *most important thing is that he was on time* for the *wedding*.

LU

That's true! Oh, dear—what time is it?

KAROLINE

It's one minute past eight!

[169]

Lu

Incredible. Half past eight and my husband isn't here yet! [WAITER *enters.*] At last, you've arrived, darling! At nine o'clock! [*Embraces him.*] What kept you so long, darling?

WAITER

I met a friend and couldn't get rid of him.

Lu

Well, sit down, darling! [*He sits in chair placed by* Lu.] No, get up and have something to drink! [*To* KAROLINE.] Give him something to drink, Karoline! [KAROLINE *gets drink from serving table.*]

WAITER

Thanks. Thanks very much.

Lu

Now come and help us a little. Let's put the chairs around the table. [KAROLINE *takes chair from R. C. and puts it at R. upper end of table.*] No, no, here! [*Indicating R. end of table.* KAROLINE *puts chair at R. end.* WAITER *puts armchair from below door L. C. to L. end of table.*] I like my guests to be seated comfortable . . . not squeezed together like sardines. There's going to be a marvelous dinner. A magnificent capon as big as an eagle. I saw him on the spit. Don't smile. There never was anything like it in your restaurant. The beer was good but the food was simply terrible! That's why you went broke. Have a cigarette. [*Hands box from table.*] You weren't born to be a restaurant proprietor. You're lucky they were willing to take you back here. Some people are born leaders, others must serve.

WAITER

If you had married me—things would have gone better!

LU

[*Arranging the table.*] Oh, don't say that! We were very wise to part while we were engaged—rather than after we were married!

WAITER

That really doesn't change matters! We parted— that's the point—and you married someone else! It was a good thing for you,—but a bad thing for me!

LU

Don't get sentimental. You'd better open the bottle instead! [WAITER *goes to serving table.*] We want to be merry tonight! Oh, dear—isn't it awful? Nine o'clock —and my husband isn't here yet!

[SPORUM *enters.*]

LU

At last, darling. Half past nine. [*She embraces him.*] Why is it that you're never on time? Where have you been so long?

SPORUM

One of my students called on me and I couldn't send him away.

[171]

Lu

When you had no money—you were always on time!

Sporum

Why not? I had nothing to do then. But now—that I'm a university professor——

Lu

[*Interrupts him.*] What's the matter with you, Max? Aren't you going to kiss your wife?

Sporum

[*Crossing to* Karoline *back of table.*] Of course I am, but you talk so much that I haven't had a chance to.
[*Kisses* Karoline.]

Karoline

Did the children go to bed?

Sporum

Yes, my angel. Don't worry, they're all asleep.

Lu

All six?

Sporum

[*Sighs.*] Yes, all six!

[172]

Lu

[*Busying herself again.*] Don't sigh, Sporum! You ought to be glad that you have a steady income and six beautiful, healthy children as well! There's nothing nicer than that! Karoline should be very proud of herself!

Karoline

And so I am! Still—it's a bit too much!

Lu

Well, when your fourth child was born—I told you to call a halt! But, lo and behold—there were two more after that!

Sporum

It was *my* fault!

Lu

Oh, I'm *sure* of *that,* my dear! [*To* Waiter.] Let me have those small glasses, please. Thanks. [*Gives glasses to* Karoline. *To* Sporum.] As you see, my former fiancé has also been invited! [Sporum *looks around.*] Sit down, Max. What are you staring at?

Sporum

It's funny—— This is the first time I've ever been in this room.

Lu

Yet it was in this room that I found you—in the telephone book! Won't you have a drop of Vermouth? [To Waiter.] Give him a glass of Vermouth? [*Takes*

drink to SPORUM, *puts arm round his neck. To* KARO-
LINE.] Oh, you're looking at my bracelet? It's my husband's anniversary present!

KAROLINE

How many diamonds are there in it?

LU

Forty small ones and five large ones! [*To* WAITER.]
Did you tell them to give my chauffeur his dinner?

WAITER

Of course.

LU

See that he gets a little champagne. But not too
much! Oh, dear—— Now I'm really upset! It's very
rude of my husband to be so late! It's half past nine!
The guests are here—and my *husband* isn't! [KONRAD
enters.] At last, darling! But it's ten o'clock. [*She embraces him.*] Why did you keep us waiting? Where have
you been?

KONRAD

I had to talk to Paris and I couldn't get through for
some time.

[*Bows to the others.*]

LU

[*Gets drink from* WAITER.] Well, have a drink, dear!
We want to be merry tonight! [*He drinks it.*] Do you
still love me?

[174]

Konrad

Always—and forever!

Lu

Then have another drink! [Lu *takes his glass back to* Waiter.] Do you love Professor Sporum, too?

Konrad

Since I have known his life's story—I am extremely fond of him! What an attractive table! And wasn't it charming of you to choose *this* room?

Lu

Do you still remember?

Konrad

Oh, don't I, though?

Lu

[*Pointing to* Waiter.] My former fiancé is also here! [Waiter *crossing to* Konrad *offers* Konrad *a Vermouth with his right hand.*]

Konrad

So,—you're head waiter here again, eh?

Waiter

Yes. But tonight—I am one of the guests!

KONRAD

Bravo!
  [*Offers to shake hands with him.* WAITER *quickly transfers glass to left hand. They shake hands.* WAITER *transfers the glass back to right hand and offers it to* KONRAD. WAITER *crosses back to serving table.*]

KONRAD

[*Drinks.*] Thanks.
  [*Goes to sofa.*]

LU

[*Busying herself again.*] So! Everything is all right now and dinner could be served—if only my husband were here! [*To* KONRAD.] You must excuse him for being late—but I'm sure he's doing something in the interests of your firm.

KONRAD

Very likely! We're lucky to have such a brilliant European Manager. We owe him to you, little *Fairy!* It was *you,* who recommended him!

LU

And it was *you,* who made him rich—so *we're quits!* But, dear me! It's half past ten! Isn't it maddening, that my *husband isn't here?*
  [DR. METZ *enters.*]

[176]

Lu

At *last, you're here!* At *eleven o'clock!* [*She embraces him.*] How *could* you be so late? Where have you been? What's been keeping you?

Metz

My secretary delayed me! There were a thousand details to be attended to! [*Mutely greets the others. Looks at his watch.*] Six minutes past eight, exactly!

Lu

Don't make excuses! You were all late! Dinner was ordered for eight o'clock sharp and it's really too bad, that my husband and guest of honor—should be the last to arrive!

Konrad

[*Jovially.*] Now look here—I can't have the "pride and joy" of my firm run down!

Lu

[*To the others.*] Ten years haven't been enough for me to teach him to be punctual! Having once been a politician—he can't get out of the habit of being late! He makes me very happy—but he's never on time! [*Kisses him.*] Do you remember this room, where you behaved so badly?

> [*They join hands and turn back to audience, looking over room.*]

[177]

METZ

How could I forget it?
[*Kisses* LU's *hand.*]

LU

I've punished you for it with ten years of marriage!

METZ

Punished me? [*To the others.*] Did you hear that? I,
who have had ten years of bliss—all of which, I owe to
my dear little wife!

LU

[*Interrupts him.*] Don't be sentimental! It's getting
late! Take your seats—— You'll find your names on the
place-cards! [LU *sits R. end of table. They sit down.
To Waiter.*] Tell your comrades outside to start serving
dinner—— [WAITER *goes to the door and gives a sig-
nal. He returns to his place and sits down.*] I hope
you're all hungry, because we're going to have *such* a
dinner! [*The stage begins to darken.*] I can say with
pride you will have a dinner . . . [*It is growing darker
rapidly.*] which I am sure will please you all. [*They
chatter merrily.*] I take all the credit for it——

> [*She continues to talk gaily. It becomes almost
> pitch dark. Nothing can be seen; only the com-
> pany's merry bantering can be heard, as the cur-
> tain falls.*]

CURTAIN

ht
2.